Mastering

the Art of the

P.A.U.S.E.

MATT WILLIAMS

Mastering the Art of the P.A.U.S.E.
© Copyright 2019 by Matt Williams

Published by: Matt Williams Ministries

ISBN: 978-0-578-48432-7

<u>Acknowledgement:</u> To my Lord and Savior, Jesus Christ, you are the sole reason I exist today. Without You, I am nothing, with You, I can do all things. To my beautiful wife, Faith, you are the love of my life. I am a better man today because of you. Thanks for keeping me grounded while still managing to allow me to spread my wings and fly. I wouldn't want to do life together with anyone else, I love you.

Contents

Introduction

Media Controls

Media. A word that we are all very familiar with in this day and age. In fact, most of the time when we hear this word, it is usually expressed in a negative way. We often hear various politicians, musical artists, actors, and even athletes express their discontent with the news media. Many of them feel like their words or statements are often misinterpreted or misconstrued by news reporters and journalists.

In general, the term *"media"* refers to various means of communication and is the main means of mass communication in our world today. Three of the main forms of media communication today are broadcasting, publishing, and the internet. These three juggernauts are responsible for producing the majority of the media outlets we have in our world today that feed us information

1

daily. Their purpose and intent are to get their message out quickly and to as many people as possible.

Broadcasting

Broadcasting media is the distribution of audio and video content, such as radio and television. It is still the most efficient way to quickly transmit information to the widest audience, although the Internet currently challenges television as the primary source of both news and recreational content.

Broadcasting originally began with AM radio around 1920. Many internet-based media-service providers like Netflix, Hulu, or Amazon Prime Video still have to rely on broadcasting to transmit their content to their viewers via television. In addition to television, radio broadcasting has become somewhat of a phenomenon in the 20th and 21st century. We, as people, rely heavily on television and radio and can access both anytime or anywhere from multiple devices, such as our phones, tablets, and computers. These major advancements in technology have certainly made accessing this form of media extremely easy and convenient.

Television and radio have revolutionized our culture and have heavily influenced the way we think, speak, act, dress, and even walk. So often we see fans who try to emulate their favorite celebrity on TV by dressing, talking, and even acting just like them. Many new fashion styles have spread across the globe through various promotional and marketing campaigns over the airwaves of the most popular radio stations. Broadcasting media has indeed had a tremendous influence on our culture.

Publishing

Publishing media is the dissemination of literature, music, or other information. Traditionally, publishing usually referred to the distribution of printed materials such as books, magazines, and newspapers. However, with the invention of digital information systems and the Internet, publishing has expanded well into electronic resources like micro-publishing, websites, blogs, and the likes. Publishing media remains one of the greatest ways for individuals to learn and retain information. Nowadays, when someone needs to learn how to do just about anything, they can usually find an article, book, magazine, video, or blog listing steps on how to do it. Quick access to valuable and knowledgeable information is often right on the edge of our fingertips.

Many companies also create songs with valuable information such as promotional deals or their phone numbers as their lyrics to ensure potential customers don't forget them. In fact, if you want someone to remember just about anything, pairing that information with a song greatly increases their chances of retaining it. Recent studies by Neuroscientists have shown that words set to music are the easiest to remember. Just think of one of the first songs we've all learned to sing: "A, B, C, D, E, F, G...Now I've sung my ABC." There is a strong link between literature and music that affects our memory. In fact, that effect is so strong that we often remember songs or commercials we don't even like!

Internet

Who would have ever thought that the internet would become as big and impactful as it is today? The internet is simply the contraction (or shrinking) of the massive groups of computer networks that are interconnected to one global system. It is often referred to as the network of networks that consists of private, public, academic, business, and government networks.

It is safe to say that virtually every organization today uses the internet in some shape or form. Much like broadcasting and publishing media platforms, the internet has revolutionized the world and our lives, whether we choose to embrace it or not. Many businesses and organizations have incorporated it into their hiring process, making it mandatory that potential candidates apply for available positions online instead of in person. Even holiday shopping traffic at physical stores has drastically decreased due to the huge uptick in online shopping. One would have to admit; the rapid advancement of the internet has created significant changes in our everyday lives. The impact the internet has on our society is felt in almost everything we do – from ordering food online to starting a romantic relationship. It has affected how we communicate, how we learn about global affairs, and even how our brains operate. Something that was once viewed as a convenience has now in many cases become a necessity for our lives.

Media-Controlled

Any organization that controls mainstream media has tremendous power over what people think, speak, and do. Such an organization can greatly influence how people perceive the world around them. Just think about all of the forms of media we encounter daily, TV, radio, internet, email, advertising posters/signs, and even messages in the workplace.

Our brains are constantly bombarded with messages. Whether consciously or subconsciously, these messages enter our minds and often influence our thoughts, become words we verbally speak, and even the very actions we take. It is no wonder millions of dollars are spent annually on commercials and other message-developing systems to deliver messages to our society. Despite how independent we often claim we are, the truth remains that we still often live with a 'monkey see, monkey do' mentality.

The government is a great example of an organization that is a major user of media. The government tries its best to communicate all kinds of messages, expressing them as beneficial to us in some sort of way. Sometimes, they are, in fact, beneficial and helpful to us. However, sadly, as with many political campaigns, the reality of promises actually being met tends to be in the lower percentage group. Nevertheless, a government using media to influence us is usually trying to control our thoughts and actions in one way or another. Whether that is a good or bad thing for our society completely depends on the motives or agenda of those in power or those pushing that very agenda.

The struggle for power and control is abundant everywhere. This is nothing new to our society at large, as mankind has always struggled and fought for control of power for centuries. The only difference in today's world is that the weapons used to influence or conquer power and control have become more technologically sophisticated.

Much like God allowed the armies of Ammon, Moab, and Mount Seir to become confused, and then start fighting amongst themselves when they came against King Jehoshaphat in II Chronicles Chapter 20, the devil is taking a similar plan and twisting it to use media in a negative light to confuse us. The devil always tries to distort, twist and defile the good and holy things of God. He has no creative power whatsoever and is one big 'ole copycat. He takes good and useful things like media and distorts them to influence us to stop following and serving God, and if he can't get us to stop following God, then he will use other media-related, time-consuming things to take our focus off of God and preoccupy us with other fruitless thoughts. He knows that if we have very little time to communicate with God, the less powerful we will eventually become as our power is rooted in God.

The devil may already be defeated; however, he is no fool by any means. He knows exactly what he is doing, and he knows how to use his weapons. He is using media as one of his biggest weapons because he understands the power of communication. Sadly, it is us who don't understand the power of communication and the strength that lies in our words. The devil knows that there is great power in the spoken word of mankind. He is very aware of the fact that we are made in the image of God and have access to the kingdom to bring heaven here on earth. It is imperative that we choose to live a life free from the control of any form of media.

Media Controls

Now that we've discussed what it means to be media-controlled, I'd like to shift gears over to media controls. In digital and analog electronics, a user interface of a me- dia device will often include buttons known as *"media controls."* In order to enact any change or adjust the process of watching a film or listening to audio, one would simply press one of these corresponding buttons. These widely known symbols are found on a multitude of software products and are often referred to as *"dominant designs."*

One of the most interesting things about dominant designs is that they are not necessarily always better than all of the other designs. They simply emerged to the front of the pack simply due to technological path-dependence and very little customer resistance regarding their design.

That's right, most dominant designs became dominant due to the sheer lack of resistance from us, the consumers. Some examples of dominant designs are common icons seen on physical devices and application software, such as media players, VCRs, DVD players, record play- ers,

remote controls, tape players, and multimedia key- boards. They are usually designed as buttons labeled as PLAY, STOP, PAUSE, REWIND, FAST-FORWARD, and RECORD.

The play button is often referred to as the play mode, normal run, or normal speed mode. When this button is pressed on a media device, that device will activate and move whatever content that is on it progressively for- ward. For example, if a device contains music or a film, once the play button is pressed, the content will begin to play or move forward at a normal speed.

The stop button or stop mode, on the other hand, means to come to an end, cease to happen or draw to a close. It is an indicator to stop the active function of a de- vice currently in the play mode. When the stop button is pressed, all current activity comes to a standstill and all progress ceases to exist. At this point, any equipment op- erating is therefore completely idle and non-progressive.

The pause button has often been thought of synonymously with the stop button. In fact, when the pause symbol was reportedly invented back in the 1960s, due to the difficulty of translating the word *"pause"* into some languages used in foreign markets, the pause symbol was designed as a variation on the existing stop button symbol.

Even though the pause button originally was created to mean a brief interruption or stutter, it somehow got lumped in with the stop button. However, the two buttons are actually quite different. Unlike stop, when the pause mode is activated, it interrupts operation intermittently, yet keeps the equipment in the operating mode (or play mode). Despite the brief interruption, the equipment is still enabled to stay active and in a productive state of mind.

The rewind button when pressed moves that which is progressing backwards, while the fast-forward button moves that which is progressing forward, faster than the normal speed (or play mode) it was currently in.

The record button is activated whenever one wants to capture a moment that they might want to refer back to or revisit at a later date. This mode is enacted simultaneously while the play mode is activated, allowing one to capture moments that are moving forward progressively in the play mode.

I'm sure by this point you're probably wondering why in the world I am taking the time to describe button functions and modes of these dominant designs that most people are already well aware of. Figuratively speaking, much like digital and analog electronics, our own lives have a user interface equipped with the media control buttons of PLAY, STOP, PAUSE, REWIND, FAST-FOR-WARD, and RECORD. In fact, we all live in these modes of life every day.

Being able to activate the rewind mode and quickly reflect on a great memory in our past thought is a blessing within itself. Being able to skip ahead suddenly in life by enabling the fast-forward mode can save us a lot of time. Or perhaps, being able to activate the record mode in our minds to mentally capture a great moment with family and friends could be one for the books, our mental photo books, that is.

The fact is, we generally decide for ourselves what buttons in life we want to press and in what mode we would like to dwell. Some of us even allow others to press our buttons for us and influence us to move into the corresponding mode that reflects the button pressed. If we are not careful, these modes could become a setback and even hindrance to us if we were to get stuck in one of them for too long, with the exception of the play and pause modes.

Being stuck in the stop, rewind, fast-forward, or record mode could be devastating. When one is stuck in the stop mode, they usually become incredibly frustrated or discouraged with their outcome in life and therefore quit or end up at a standstill.

If one is stuck in the rewind mode, they will often live life in the rearview mirror, thinking about what could've, should've, or would've been accomplished had the outcome been just a little different.

Being stuck in the fast-forward mode can influence one to live life day-dreaming so far into the future that they forget to enjoy and appreciate living their life in the play mode or present mode of life.

Or perhaps, one finds themselves stuck in the record mode, so caught up on hoarding and capturing the present moments in the play mode that they overlook the opportunity to live in *the now* and continue to create new moments. Whatever the case might be, being stuck too long in any mode other than the play and pause mode can present significant issues if one is not careful.

Life circumstances have influenced many of us to move outside of the play mode and into another mode of life. Some of us have had some very tragic and justifiable experiences, ending up stuck in the stop mode or any mode other than play or pause. Staying in the play mode requires much discipline and grit and can be a daunting task when faced with a tragedy. However, even in the midst of our tragedy, does God want us to be stuck any-where? Does He want us to be stuck in a mode of life that would cause us to be idle or move into a mode that is not at our normal speed of life? I have a feeling you already know the answers to those questions. In this book, you will learn sound Biblical principles to ensure that you keep leaving your life in a progressive state of mind, known as the play mode.

After reading this book, once conflict arises, you would know exactly what to do. Are you ready to live your life predominantly in the play mode? If so, let's go deeper!

Chapter 1

The Play Mode

▶

"Brethren, I do not count myself to have apprehended; but one thing I do, forgetting those things that are behind and reaching forward to those things which are ahead, I press toward the goal for the prize of the upward call of God in Christ Jesus." - Philippians 3:13-14

In popular culture, the play button is arguably the most widely used of the media control symbols. This makes sense, considering the fact that the play mode is where normal activity, action, speed, or movement takes place. The play mode is a place where one can listen to audio or watch a film at a controlled, yet normal speed. It is a place where all of the activity of media communication progressively moves forward. It is a vibrant mode, full of life, excitement, and movement.

The play mode is more normal and natural for us than we think. In the beginning, when God created the heavens and the earth, the Bible says that the earth was without form and void. It wasn't until God spoke the famous words, *"Let there be light"* that the earth started to take its form, shape, and even rotate. God pressed the figurative play button on the world known to us as *"Earth."*

In the Beginning

From the beginning of time, all the way up until this present time, our world has been in play mode. Life is in motion, and the motion picture of life is being played at normal speed. However, that normal speed is indeed an incredibly fast speed. As schoolchildren, you may have learned that earth is moving around the sun at a speed of 67,000 miles per hour. In addition, the earth whirls around the center of our galaxy at 490,000 miles per hour. No wonder this world often causes our heads to spin! I'm kidding.

In all seriousness, however, the point I'm trying to make is that this earth and virtually everything in it was created to move. For example, 71 percent of the Earth is covered with water. The oceans alone hold 96.5 percent of Earth's water. Water is constantly in the play mode known as a process we call *"the water cycle."* This cycle is a continuous movement of water on, above, and below Earth's surface. Water moves from one place to another, such as from a river to ocean, or from the ocean to the atmosphere, by the various processes of evaporation, precipitation, condensation, infiltration, surface runoff, and subsurface flow. During its movement, water goes through different forms: liquid, solid (ice), and vapor. When water evaporates, it takes up energy. When it condenses, it releases energy and warms the environment. It is during these heat exchanges that climate is influenced and reacts to what we call *"climate changes."* In other words, the climate then becomes on the move. Movement, as you see, is completely natural and, in some cases, necessary.

Born to Move

Much like water, we were born to influence our climate in life. However, we were not created to solely influence our climate to benefit ourselves; we are to influence our climate for the Kingdom of God. Movement or motion is necessary if we plan to make a difference in this world. Sitting idly, watching life going by is a recipe for disaster, disappointment, and ultimately failure.

Our bodies can contribute to this world not only by our physical movement but also by the way we move mentally. The body is thoroughly involved in our thought processes, understanding, emotions, and decision-making. The mind and the body are inseparable.

Daniel Wolpert, a British medical doctor, once said: "We have a brain for one reason and one reason only, and that's to produce adaptable and complex movements." Our spirit is to receive messages or information from God. However, our brains are responsible for processing those messages or information into a way that eventually forms movement from our bodies. God loves movement. He never changes; however, He loves to move.

When we press the figurative play button on our lives, we start to forge the path toward our destiny. God said in Jeremiah 29:11 (NIV), "For I know the plans I have for you," declares the Lord, "plans to prosper you and not to harm you, plans to give you hope and a future." He also said in Jeremiah Chapter 1, that before He formed us in the belly of our mother, He knew us and set us apart to fulfill our destiny.

Our life has already been created, formed, and written. God is the author, editor, producer, and director of our lives. He has pressed the figurative play button on our lives and has placed us in the play mode. It is completely up to us to decide whether or not we stay in play mode, or whether we allow a media-controlled life, or a life controlled by outsiders to influence us to move into another mode outside of God's will. God allows us to choose and make our own choice. He is that loving of a God and that secure in Himself that He allows us the wonderful freedom of choice or free-will. However, it is important for us to always remember that He is the author of our lives. Therefore, He knows the path we need to take to receive the wonderfully progressive life He has already prepared for us.

Life in the Play Mode

The word *"play"* means to engage in an activity for enjoyment. It means to amuse oneself, entertain oneself, or enjoy oneself. Our lives are meant to be full of enjoyment. They were never created to be only playful later in life during retirement. Life should be filled with laughter, amusement, entertainment, and productivity, now AND in retirement. Christ came to earth so that we might have life and have it more abundantly.

Sure, being debt-free and saving money for retirement is smart and financially responsible; I totally support and practice those very ideas myself. We should always be practical about using and enjoying some money now and putting the rest away for a rainy day and retirement. However, I'm not talking just about money. People

19

who think money will answer all of their problems and give them purpose are usually the ones that don't have enough of it. Money solves a lot of issues in the physical, but it does very little for us in the mental and spiritual state of mind. In fact, when is having enough money really ever enough? At some point, we have to decide at what level we choose to be content with our lives and when enough is enough. That answer is completely dependent upon us and what our preference is regarding our own ideal lifestyle.

The play mode is not an actual physical place but is a mindset or an established set of attitudes held by someone who desires to live a peaceful, yet successfully, productive life. It is a place of being active, operative, and effective. It is an environment where creativity is born and thrives. It is a place where the motion picture of life (our dreams, goals, and purpose) are accomplished and fulfilled. It is a place where we all should strive to predominantly remain.

I say predominantly remain, due to the reality that we cannot live our lives always in the play mode without ever needing to enact another mode periodically. In fact, these other modes are a blessing if used correctly and activated at the right time.

The play mode is not a perfect place. There's no such thing as a perfect place in life. Life has moments of interruption and seasons of extreme difficulty. Even though it was originally designed to be a perfect place, the fact of the matter remains; this world is far from perfect. The truth is, much like a CD, record, cassette, or videotape, our lives can still be damaged, scratched, beaten up, or even worse case, broken.

As a kid, you may have heard the expression, *"Sticks and stones may break my bones, but words will never hurt me."* Though the intent was meant well, this expression could not be further from the truth. The truth is, words do hurt us. In fact, words often hurt us much more than physical abuse does, and often have much longer lingering effects.

Some of us may have forgotten a past physical altercation we were involved in. However, many of us have never forgotten the abusive words that someone had spoken to us. Think about the grudge or resentment you might have carried for days, weeks, months or even years in some cases. How did that offense affect you? Did you really have peace? Sure, some negative words that have been spoken might have in exchange, motivated you to accomplish a specific goal. However, even then, wasn't there still a price to pay? Wasn't there still an emotional or mental scar left on our soul or at least in your mind?

21

Did you really have peace throughout that entire process of striving to reach your goal? It is true, we cannot prevent others from saying something to us, but we can prevent reacting in a negative way. Many people have no filter on their mouths and are often going to say whatever they want. However, we can choose how we respond. We can choose whether or not we stay in the play mode mindset of life or move out of it into another mode.

Rewind & Fast-Forward Mode

In life, we can experience sudden circumstances that set us back or sudden circumstances that catapult us forward. In some cases, the forward catapult experience might place us in a position where we feel we don't deserve, or we are not qualified for yet. Whether we receive an award from a project we hardly worked on or get promoted to a career position we lack qualifications or experience for, life has a way of being very generous to us sometimes; much more than we probably care to admit. However, life also has its sudden jolts or bumps that can quickly derail us if we are not careful while traveling down its path. I refer to these two modes in life as the rewind and fast-forward mode.

The rewind mode usually reflects a setback or the repeating of a past experience. This mode is usually activated when an experience from the present is missed or overlooked and now becomes part of history. When one desires to recall that very experience, they would typically press the rewind button and activate the rewind mode. This function will then bring a memory of the past experience into the present time, known as you guessed it, the play mode.

A memory is a copy, an image, or a recollection of something that is real. It is not the actual real thing or real experience. Bringing an actual experience from the past into the present time is impossible. Unless we are God, it cannot be done. We can bring physical things from the past into the future, but we cannot bring past experiences. They are stuck in the past forever. It is amazing how many people try to relive their past experiences in the present mode of life — so many live their lives through the view of a rearview mirror instead of a front windshield. Not many of us would drive our cars only looking through the rearview mirrors. However, so many of us live our lives that way.

What is interesting about the front windshield of a car is that it is made to shield wind. Not only does it shield wind, but it also shields small rocks and road debris from hitting us. When we choose to live life in the play mode, we choose to live life God's way. We choose to travel forward behind the front windshield He has prepared for us to shield life's wind, small rocks and road debris that so easily causes others to stumble.

The rewind mode function is a great feature if something important was overlooked or something valuable was temporarily misplaced. However, unfortunately, the rewind mode does not have the capability to filter memories. This is always the danger of visiting the past in the rewind mode for too long. If one is not careful, he or she could end up right back at where they started. Sometimes, memories in the rewind mode can become very cloudy. Because we are in an abnormal mode, identifying memories in their proper order or perspective can be quite a challenge. In fact, many memories can be mixed with others, and that memory is mistaken for a completely different date, and in some cases, a completely different location.

The rewind mode can be a dangerous place if one is not careful. The Apostle Paul understood this when he said in Philippians 3:14-16 (NKJV), "Brethren, I do not count myself to have apprehended; but one thing I do, forgetting those things that are behind and reaching forward to those things which are ahead. I press toward the goal for the prize of the upward call of God in Christ Jesus."

Are you moving forward and pressing towards your goals? Are you consistently living life in the play mode or are you looking in the rear-view mirror of life dwelling on the past? Make it a point not to live your life stuck in the rewind mode. Make it a point to live life looking forward towards your goals and not backwards dwelling on past experiences. It's fool's gold; we can't change our past experiences no matter how hard we try.

When the fast-forward media control button is figuratively pressed in life, its activation will move someone quickly ahead; much faster than they would normally move in the play mode. Whether this mode is a blessing or a curse totally depends on the person's situation. If one is diligent at learning valuable lessons from past experiences, one may simply press the figurative fast-forward button of life and skip forward. This function will then briefly push them ahead until they reach an area in life that they have not yet conquered. In fact, God is notorious for moving people ahead suddenly once they have learned life's valuable lessons. When this happens, one can rejoice, as that usually means God has certified and ordained them for that particular season. Which also means He has equipped them with new skills and a new grace to accomplish the task. What a mighty God we serve!

A slight problem with the fast-forward mode, however, is much like the rewind mode, we can also choose to get stuck there or even worse, move forward prematurely. There is nothing worse than the sight of someone in a position that they are not qualified to occupy. All of us know someone that was promoted far too soon. When we move forward too soon, we often leave behind valuable information that we could have learned to help guide us in our future, or in this case, our new present time. When such a situation occurs, the results are often disastrous. Being stuck in the fast-forward mode of life is just as dangerous as being stuck in the rewind mode. However, it is a great mode to experience when used correctly.

The Record Mode

The record mode, as stated in the introduction, is a mode that can only be enabled within the play mode. It cannot be enabled within any other mode other than play. It cannot be enabled in the stop, pause, rewind or fast-forward mode. It can only be enabled in the play mode.

The record mode is meant to primarily capture things in motion instead of things that are typically stagnant. It feeds off of forward motion or progress. In fact, even though the record mode can capture an experience or an image that is not moving, it still must be enabled within the play mode, which is, of course, moving in itself. Sure, there is a time to appreciate the experience of still images, such as fancy art collections and historical artifacts. However, if we are honest enough to admit it, though extraordinary, still images don't create quite the excitement, energy, or buzz of something else that is in motion.

Visiting a museum and then visiting an amusement park are two completely different experiences. Life is like an amusement park: there's usually a lot of people around; traffic when we come and go; we have to wait our turn to enjoy certain rides; some experiences bring us great joy and laughter; other experiences freak us out terribly, almost give us a heart attack, or even worse, make us nearly wet our pants; there's great food to enjoy along the way, and there's souvenirs to collect to remind us of the experience. Life is one big rollercoaster full of ups and downs, loops and turns, climbing and falling. It is up to us to decide what type of experience we are going to ultimately have before the ride comes to an end. We have to decide if we will enjoy it to the fullest or cry and complain the entire time.

Our brains are walking cameras, and our eyes are the camera's lenses. In fact, studies have shown that camera lenses operate very similarly to our eyes and vice-versa. Our brain acts like the film or the memory card storing images away, while our eyes capture the images of the activities we experience. In fact, our brains can store over one million gigabytes worth of information! That's more than 30,000 times the capacity of the average memory card!

One of the most fascinating things about our brains is that they are always recording and capturing experiences subconsciously. Unlike a user interface that can only record in play mode, our brains record 24 hours a day, 365 days a year, regardless of what mode we find ourselves in. I believe God designed us like this for a reason. He is an intentional God and does everything by design and through calculated movements. I believe God allows us to remember all of our bad experiences so we can appreciate the good. I believe He allows us to reflect on the past so that we can cherish the good times and learn valuable lessons from the not-so-good. Our memories are meant to serve us in a positive way, not a negative way. It is the trick of the enemy that confuses us by reminding us of the negative memories of our past, which brings us guilt and shame. However, we are to resist the urge to yield to these thoughts. We must do our best to focus on the positive and live our life predominately in the play mode. Paul said in Philippians 4:8 (NKJV), "Finally, brethren, whatever things are true, whatever things are noble, whatever things are just, whatever things are pure, whatever things are lovely, whatever things are of good report, if there is any virtue and if there is anything praiseworthy—meditate on these things." I totally concur with Paul and you should too. Living your life in the play mode is completely up to you. Make a decision today that you will place yourself in a position to experience God's best for your life. Move back into the play mode.

Chapter 2

The Stop Mode

"There is no fear in love; but perfect love casts out fear, because fear involves torment." - 1 John 4:18 (NKJV)

Have you ever felt like everyone was moving forward—except you? Have you ever felt like just about everyone around you was either getting married, starting a family, advancing in their careers, making more money, taking vacations, but you were still stagnant? Perhaps you feel like that now. If so, trust me, you are not alone. Many others (including myself) have been in your shoes. I too have struggled with the thought of life passing me by or the thought that maybe I've already missed my opportunity in life. I too have had seasons of depression where I've felt like a failure or inadequate. These dark seasons of life can influence many of us to lose hope and give up on our dreams. Fighting depression is a real battle, and if one is not careful, they will find their life at a complete standstill or even worse, stagnant.

Stagnant Water

The word *"stagnant"* means still, motionless, immobile, lifeless, dead, stationary, slow-moving, declining, dying, depressed, and dormant, just to name a few. Stagnation is never a good thing for our lives. Our bodies rely and thrive on movement. They are made to move and flow much like water. For example, water that is stagnant has stopped flowing in its normal mode or speed. When this happens, it can become a major environmental hazard.

Stagnant water usually becomes a breeding ground for mosquitoes that transmit diseases such as malaria and the dengue virus. It also can be dangerous to drink due to the growth of algae, bacteria, and parasites. Human and animal feces often are found in stagnant water, particularly in deserts and other areas of low rain. This type of water becomes infected with bacteria and diseases it would normally seldom encounter if it remained in motion or flowing.

Much like water, when our lives become stagnant or motionless, we become a major hazard to our own environment. Our lack of forward progress will often create stress, frustration, jealousy, which eventually gives birth to bitterness. Our attitudes then become toxic, and our comments are often expressed through bitterness, resentment, or even sarcasm.

Sarcasm in particular, on the surface, seems like the most harmless of the three because we often use it in a joking way. However, most people who are heavily sarcastic or use sarcasm in a way to make someone feel inferior are usually threatened by that individual. In fact, one of the roots of sarcasm is jealousy; they both are connected.

Jealousy is very similar to bacteria. Just as bacteria lives in symbiotic and parasitic relationships with plants and animals, jealousy that is unchecked can also live inside of us. When this happens, it will breed hatred, which will then give birth to all sorts of conflict in our lives.

One must be very careful and diligent when it comes to using sarcasm. It often can run much deeper than a light-hearted joke; there could be an underlying issue of jealousy also present. Don't allow spiritual bacteria to fester inside of you and contaminate the spiritual living water that dwells within your soul. Let your spirit flow like rivers of living water, being a blessing to all of whom you come in contact with.

Did you know that the adult human body weight contains about 60 percent of water? Water is of importance to all living creatures. In fact, some organisms have a much higher percentage of water body weight than ours, such as babies and small children. Water is made to move and flow through our bodies, and when it does, it serves a number of essential functions to keep us going: It helps regulate internal body temperature by sweating and respiration; It transports carbohydrates and proteins our bodies use as food through the water in the bloodstream; It assists in flushing wastes in our bodies through urination; It forms saliva; It lubricates joints. Finally, it acts as a shock absorber for the brain, spinal cord, and fetus.

In addition to water, our bodies have several internal systems such as: A circulatory system, digestive system, endocrine system, immune system, lymphatic system, muscular system, nervous system, reproductive system, respiratory system, skeletal system, and urinary system, all which involve movement. Each one of these systems helps the human body function properly by sending, receiving, producing, expanding, contracting, or even processing something our bodies need in order to keep moving.

Still in the Stop Mode

Negative life circumstances have persuaded many of us to press the figurative stop button on our lives and become stagnant and at a standstill. There are many people in life that are physically alive, yet spiritually dead. They might be physically moving; nevertheless, they are *still in the stop mode*. When I use the word "still" in this phrase, I mean still as in not moving or motionless. People who are *still in the stop mode* are people who are not moving or are motionless. They are usually battling fear, stress, frustration, tension, nervousness, and agitation, also known as inner anxiety.

The word *"stop"* means ceasing, terminating, ending, finishing, or standstill. It means to give up, quit, leave off, knock off, abandon, or to refuse to move or operate. This mode of life is often activated when we allow our inner anxieties to get the best of us. However, this is a mode that we should desperately try to avoid at all costs. Much like stagnant water, when we are in a stagnant position, we are in an unhealthy place; an unhealthy place I call the stop mode.

Inner Anxiety

Mass media has had a huge influence on our thoughts

and actions as a whole. Some of the influences communicated through mass media may initially be viewed in a positive light. However, if one is not careful to filter their thoughts and desires for these same things, they could be eventually overtaken by inner anxiety if these things are not received in a timely fashion. A prime example would be when we see a celebrity or public figure obtain or accomplish a goal on TV that we desire for ourselves as well. If not filtered, we could have thoughts of jealousy or become envious of them if our own lives do not reflect those same desired outcomes. Failure to reach the same results can influence us to become full of hatred, discouraged or downright depressed when life doesn't work the way for us as it has for someone else.

Inner anxiety has a way of making us feel prematurely defeated or ready to quit on a task before the outcome is even decided. It is launched as an attack on our minds. It is a battle that goes on right between our ears. The sound of that battle can become so loud that one will struggle to hear themselves think clearly, let alone hear God trying to communicate with them. That is why monitoring what we feed our minds is so important. There is always a reaction from our bodies, according to what we feed ourselves. If we eat good, we feel good. If we eat bad, our bodies pay for it. One would simply need to complete the Daniel Fast to confirm this truth. What we feed our-selves matters. We are whoever we think we are; how-ever, we feel like the things we digest.

When it comes to what we feed our bodies through the various channels of media, whatever we feed our-selves will grow. Do you really think big companies spend millions of dollars on advertisements solely be-cause they love their brands that much? Of course not! They do it because they have researched and found that the effective use of traditional media has brought them great financial success by reaching their targeted audi-ence and influencing them to purchase their promoted products.

Big brands are not successful solely because of the high quality of their products and customer service. Even though these attributes are highly important to their suc-cess, these things are still not their greatest weapons. Their greatest weapon is their ability to penetrate and in-fluence your mind through advertising. The way these companies persuasively communicate their brands to us in the marketplace is the exact thing that ultimately drives their sales revenue. Slogans like, "Just Do It," "Have It Your Way," "Eat Fresh," "Finger-Lickin' Good," or "They're GR-R-R-reat!" are all communicating messages to us that companies hope will prompt and compel us into action. These companies are strategic in conveying the message to their customers that their product is the best option in the marketplace, even if there are more inexpensive options out there. Talk about a return on investment!

There is nothing wrong with these businesses promoting their products and services. That is not my point. The point I am trying to make is that everything that enters our mind, body, and soul must be filtered. If we fail to do this, we leave ourselves wide open for the enemy to use these same strategies to launch sneak attacks on our lives and relationships. So many bad deals have been done on impulsive or careless behavior. The fear of missing out is a real struggle for some and has cost many a great price.

Inner anxiety or fear is a condition that starts by affecting an individual first. Once that individual has been fully consumed with inner anxiety, it will eventually begin to leak out of their spiritual pores, spreading onto others. Have you ever been around someone that expressed a particular fear or concern for something, then all of a sudden, you started to have the same fearful thoughts or concerns? It is a very contagious condition and is not usually satisfied until it has produced inner anxiety inside of everyone it comes in contact with.

Anxiety is a weapon the devil uses to keep God's children in bondage. The devil strives very hard to keep us living in fear, frustration, guilt, and shame. He knows that a life filled with anxiety is a life filled without love. A life without love is a life without God for God is love. The Bible says in 1 John 4:18 (NKJV), "There is no fear in love, but perfect love casts out fear because fear involves torment."

Many people allow the devil to torment them. They allow him to lie to them about their personal lives, their marriages, their families, their health, and even their destiny. God does not want us to feel tormented. I say *"feel tormented"* because the devil cannot torment followers of Christ on his own power. Believers cannot be demon-possessed or experience demonic possession unless we allow the devil to enter our bodies by denouncing Christ. The Bible clearly states that where the Spirit of the Lord is, there is liberty, not captivity. Why let the devil torment you? Stop giving him the authority to do such a thing!

The devil is a powerless enemy and cannot do any physical harm to us unless God allows it. In the book of Job, the devil had to ask God for His permission to afflict Job. Satan is liked a chained-up, aggressively barking dog. Unless that dog is let loose, he is of no threat to us as we walk by. Why then aren't you walking? Why be afraid to walk the path God has chosen for you? The devil's greatest weapon is to lie to us, creating inner anxiety, and then influence us to move from the play mode into the stop mode. He can't make us do anything; we do it to ourselves. We give him power over our lives. It's time to take back your power!

Ironically, the devil was the chief musician in heaven before he was expelled. He is well aware of media controls and how to press our buttons in life. He studies us and knows exactly what we like and what we don't like. He knows what upsets us, and he knows what lures us back into sin. Most of all, he knows what we fear, and he knows how to use that fear against us to cause us to stop progress in our lives.

When a TV, radio, cell phone, or computer has a bad network connection, the audio or video of that device will usually become distorted and hard to see. Eventually, the device may start to buffer, skip, or even worse, disconnect from the network, leaving the screen blank and full of white noise. The sound of white noise is often so piercing of a sound that rather than fixing the network issue, one will instead turn off the device out of sheer frustration or annoyance. What is the sound of the white noise in your life? What static or unclear picture is the devil influencing you to hear or see? What is he telling you about yourself?

What is he whispering in your ear as an attempt to discourage you? If you stop listening, he will eventually stop talking. The Bible says if you resist him, he will eventually flee. The devil hates patient people. He has the patience of a toddler. However, God is patient and calculated. He doesn't rush anything. He doesn't need to rush because He is God and God alone. Whatever He says He will do, He will do. He loves to do great things for those that love Him. So, if you love Him, why are you rushing your life? Rest in His love. Never forget that the kingdom of Heaven is our network and God is our provider. We can tap into our network at any time and have faith that God will give us whatever we ask for.

When we are connected with God and walking in His purpose for our lives (also known as the play mode), our vision and hearing become clearer. God's connection is never interrupted unless we sabotage that connection ourselves through sin. His network is impenetrable unless He grants access. God desires for us to know His will for our lives. He wants us to fulfill our destiny. He is not hiding it from us or trying to make us earn it through our good deeds. We could never earn His love. We could never earn our purpose or calling. He has already freely given it to us through His grace. All we have to do is muster up enough faith to ask Him to show us His plan for our lives. After we pray that prayer, our next step is to get up and move and have complete trust that He is ordering our steps and guiding us down the right path. There comes a point in life when we have to stop letting our own fears and inner anxiety rob us of God's blessings for our lives.

Uneasiness, agitation, stress, and tension usually occur when we don't feel happy about where we are in life. Some of us may feel like we should be further along in life or more accomplished. Others may feel like their relationship or family dynamic is somewhat out of sync. Truth is, if we continue to allow these feelings to develop and harbor inside of us without filtering out the white noise, outward conflict will eventually manifest itself in our lives.

Outward Conflict

The creation of steam is an interesting topic to study. Steam is usually produced when a device such as a boiler or steam generator compresses water and then applies heat energy to it. The boiler or generator acts as a firebox or furnace in order to burn fuel and generate heat. The generated heat is then transferred to water, bringing it to boil, which eventually produces steam.

Life in this world acts much like a boiler or generator. It has a way of making us feel compressed, bottled in, or even suppressed at times. It is easy to feel as if we are competing for first place in a rat-race or living our lives in vain as if there is no real meaning in what we do. We too can feel like water trapped inside of a boiler or generator waiting for the heat or pressure to be applied. We too can start to boil with our own steam of life.

Steam in its purest form is not a bad thing; on the contrary, steam when pure and properly channeled can iron out a lot of wrinkles in our lives (pun intended). It can power machinery, help cleanse our skin, soothe and relax the body, and even help us breathe better, just to name a few. However, on the other hand, improperly channeled or contaminated steam can cause severe injury, and in some cases, fatal results.

Life happens and will continue to happen to all of us, regardless of what we do. However, choosing to stop and sit by idly only allows the living water inside of you to become contaminated due to your stagnation. When this happens, the heat and pressure of this world will eventually bring you to a boil. If the steam you produce at this point is not channeled properly, or even worse, contaminated, outward conflict is sure to negatively affect you and others around you. How many people do you know that have become contaminated with inner anxiety, and as a result, lash out on people often? How many people do you know that struggle with anger issues? I submit to you that there is a deeper reason behind it than them just being angry about their current situation. The Bible says, "Be angry, and do not sin." In other words, the release of steam (or anger) is fine as long as it is properly channeled and controlled. However, the release of contaminated steam (or sin) is never acceptable and should be dealt with immediately.

Unhandled or contaminated steam creates burns and causes many people around it to become severely hurt. Jesus said in Luke 8:17 (NKJV), "For nothing is secret that will not be revealed, nor anything hidden that will not be known and come to light." Any contaminated thoughts that we have internally will eventually become an outward expression leading to an outward conflict. A sudden outward conflict that we are not prepared for can catch us off guard, and as a result, cause us to become full of inner anxiety. When our inner anxiety pressures us beyond our limits, we typically press the figurative stop button on our lives, causing us to quit, flee, shutdown, or even worse, become combative. Our inner anxiety at this point will usually help us foster outward conflict.

None of the above reactions are ever progressive or productive, yet, they seem to be our go-to method in the time of crisis. They often interrupt our lives and cause us to stop doing all of the other activities we normally do so well. Instead, we once again become motionless, stagnant, and at a standstill. How many times have you seen an offended person walk away from a team or project? How many dynasties have broken up or have separated due to conflict? How many relationships have been destroyed beyond repair out of frustration or a silly misunderstanding? Inner Anxiety is a battle waged on your mind by the devil in an attempt to convince you to self-sabotage your destiny. The devil wants to download inner anxiety into your mind so that you, in return, will produce negative outward actions. The devil wants to kill your spirit, steal your joy, and destroy your peace. It's time to fight back and retain the blessings God has given you!

Creating conflict is one of the devil's oldest yet greatest tricks. God is not the author of confusion; the devil is. It is his favorite weapon to use to interrupt our communication with God and others. He loves to confuse us through his lies. In fact, Jesus called him "The father of lies" (John 8:44 NIV). Lies are all he knows how to father and they are his children. Only a bad father would use his children for evil. Don't allow the devil to impregnate your dreams with his children of lies. Don't fall for his trap. In fact, if the devil is usually talking, he is usually lying.

The fact is, if we reject the lies, we will have a different perspective on the heat and pressure we experience in life. We often view heat and pressure as bad things; nonetheless, some of the greatest things in this world are created from heat and pressure. For example, diamonds are crystals of pure carbon that have been created from a combination of high temperatures and extreme pressure in Earth's mantle. Who doesn't love diamonds? Are they considered of value in today's world? You bet they are, and so are you! This world is known to create great heat and pressure. Heat or pressure in itself is not necessarily an issue. How we view and handle both is the true determining factor of our success in life.

The earth's crust is like a pressure cooker. The world that we live in today is no different. People continue to compartmentalize their inner anxieties until they eventually explode and spill out when real heat and pressure is applied.

Earth's minerals typically do not form well under standard conditions. They perform well once high temperatures and pressure are applied to them. Our bodies are no different. In fact, our bodies are also filled with our own minerals that support us, such as calcium, potassium, sodium, magnesium, phosphorus, chloride, and other trace minerals. Usually, we don't realize we lack potassium until we get cramps in our bodies from high-energy exercise. We hardly realize that we are low on calcium until outside weight or pressure is applied to our bones, making them feel pain or slightly brittle. We seldom realize how important sodium is until we sweat it out of our body's pores, leaving us with a sense of thirst and dehydration. However, when we have the right dosage of these minerals inside of our bodies, when heat or pressure is applied, these minerals rise up inside of us and respond to support our bodies. It is when the body is most threatened by an outside source that these minerals truly come alive inside of us.

When we cast out inner anxiety, and we instead fill ourselves with the Holy Spirit, He rises to the occasion to help us overcome the devil's attacks. He is ready to comfort and guide us through any and every situation we face or encounter. He is ready to encourage us and remind us of who we really are and whose we really are. When the heat and pressures of this life come our way, we can be convinced in our minds that God is using that same heat and pressure to form us into diamonds! The devil means it for evil, but God is faithful enough to turn it around for our good. Shine bright and be a light to this dark and lost world. Shine bright like the diamond that you are!

Chapter 3

The P.A.U.S.E. Mode

(II)

"Be anxious for nothing, but in everything by prayer and supplication, with thanksgiving, let your requests be made known to God; and the peace of God, which surpasses all understanding, will guard your hearts and minds through Christ Jesus." - Philippians 4:6-7 (NKJV)

In digital and analog electronics, a media player user interface will often include a media control button called *"pause."* The pause button (or pause mode) is a brief interruption that places the operation of a device that is currently in play mode on hold intermittently while keeping that device in operating mode. Unlike the stop mode, when the pause mode is activated, it allows a user to briefly hold the content in play mode in its current position without bringing that content to a full stoppage.

When the user is then ready to proceed, he or she simply needs to press the play button again, enabling the play mode and allowing the content to move forward once again.

Typically, if a user were to press the stop button on a device instead of the pause button, he or she would have to start the play mode over again from the beginning once he or she chose to resume progress. One could see the huge benefit in saving precious time when using the pause button in oppose to the stop button. When one does not wish to stop the content they are enjoying and then start it all over, the pause button function can indeed be a true lifesaver.

Conflict that arises in our lives often causes an interruption to our normal mode or speed of life known again as the play mode. Unfortunately, we cannot prevent conflict from entering our lives. There is nothing we can do to ensure that we never encounter a problem, dispute, or argument. We can take steps to minimize them, but we cannot eliminate them completely from happening. As life continues to happen, conflict will continue to arise. In fact, many of us would not appreciate the good experiences in life if we lived a life without conflict.

Conflict is a symptom of this sick and fallen world. When conflict arises in our lives and causes us to interrupt our progress in the play mode, we usually have two choices: 1) Press stop or, 2) Press pause. We learned in the last chapter the downsides of living life in the stop mode. However, what about pressing the pause button when conflict arises? Other than maintaining your current position, how does taking this brief break really present a better option than the stop mode? I'm glad you asked. Let's dive in a little deeper and see.

Mastering the Art of the P.A.U.S.E. is more than just taking the time to pause during a conflict. Though that is the first thing you should do during conflict, there is more to the P.A.U.S.E. than you think. When conflict arises, you have probably heard that it is a good idea to pause. What you have not heard yet is that it is a good idea to "P.A.U.S.E."

P.A.U.S.E. is actually an acronym which consists of the following five steps: *Probe, Ask, Unlock, Suggest,* and *Evaluate.* P.A.U.S.E. is founded in the Bible scripture in Philippians 4:6-7 (NKJV), which says, "Be anxious for nothing, but in everything by prayer and supplication, with thanksgiving, let your requests be made known to God; and the peace of God, which surpasses all understanding, will guard your hearts and minds through

Christ Jesus." In the next few chapters, we will discuss and breakdown this scripture in great detail, as well as discuss what each letter in this acronym means and how to apply it. However, let's first discuss the concept behind the P.A.U.S.E. mode and how to apply it.

The Challenges of Taking a Break or Time-Out

"Let's just Stop!" "Enough already!" "Let's take a time-out!" "I think we need to take a break!" "I'll be back later!" "I want a divorce!" Sadly, all of these phrases promote a conversation to stop, cease, or end. What is even sadder is the many relationships that have ended and have never recovered after some of these infamous words above were expressed during a conflict.

In the heat of an exchange, these words will usually give us time to get off the crazy train and temporarily stop an argument. However, is stopping really the solution, or is our ability to properly assess and resolve the conflict at hand the real solution? Are the above phrases or statements what we really mean, or are they words we merely express due to the frustration of running out of helpful solutions?

Look, I get it. Usually, people say these phrases to prevent the situation from escalating further or to maintain whatever peace is left between the two parties. I get that, and to an extent, I agree with that method, as long as the stoppage is brief. However, the problem is, most people who often use these phrases during an argument are already at a point where the two little devils of inner anxiety and outward conflict have gotten the best of them. From there, the only thing left to do at this point to salvage any remaining sanity is to stop, regroup, reload, and try again at a later time. When this happens, the stoppage is usually anything but brief. The intent to reconcile might be there initially, however, more often than not, when a conflict has already gone this far, offense, judgment, frustration, disrespect, and unloving comments or actions have usually already occurred; making the outcome anything but easy to resolve.

The challenge with the "time-out" or "take a break" solution is that as time passes with an unresolved issue, the devil goes to work on our hearts and minds. He starts to whisper negative thoughts into our heads. He starts to lie to us about what the other person really meant or what their real intent behind their words or actions were. The longer we carry this burden, the harder our hearts become. A hardened heart is almost impossible to penetrate at this point. If you're fortunate enough, you will be able to ask the other party to pray about it, leave it to God, and believe Him for a resolution before the situation has gotten too far out of control. However, if you're anything like me, chances are your situation might have gotten past this point already. Figuring out how to win round two was usually my game plan. Thank God for deliverance, and thank God that there is another way!

The Apostle Paul experienced his own conflict firsthand when he had a heated exchange with Barnabas in the Bible in Acts, Chapter 15. Paul and Barnabas wanted to visit some of their brethren in a few cities they had visited and preached in previously. The Bible says Barnabas was determined to take his cousin with him, named John Mark; yes, the same Mark that wrote the book of Mark. However, Paul resisted and insisted that John Mark stay behind because he had abandoned them on a previous mission. At this point, the Bible says the contention became so sharp between Paul and Barnabas that they parted from one another. Barnabas took Mark and sailed to Cyprus, but Paul chose another gentleman named Silas and departed for Syria and Cilicia. Granted, we don't know for certain whether or not Paul and Barnabas ever worked together again. However, what we do know is that they were never recorded together again in scripture after this dispute. What is even more interesting is the fact that Paul eventually ended up working with

John Mark again later after the dispute; yes, the very one they were arguing about in the first place!

I believe the devil used the John Mark debate as a weapon to trip up Paul and Barnabas and ultimately separate them. The devil is great at making us think that something is a big deal when in all actuality, it isn't. Before we know it, we are arguing over something that seems so meaningless or minuscule. It is because of our own pride that we often cannot let the subject go, and even worse, end up separating over it. Separating us is really what the devil is after. We'll never know how many great feats Paul and Barnabas might have accomplished had they both stayed and did ministry and life together. Their full potential working together will never be realized. If only they took the time to P.A.U.S.E.

Studies have shown that resolving conflict quickly has a much higher success rate than taking an extended period of time off before returning to resolve a conflict. One of my favorite shows to watch on TV is called *"The First 48."* It is a show about police detectives from major cities racing against the clock to solve homicides within the first 48 hours the homicide occurs. The reason these detectives move so quickly is due to studies showing that if they don't find a lead within the first 48 hours, their chances of solving the case are cut into half. Witnesses' recollection of the events starts to become hazy, suspects have usually fled town by then, or crime scenes and evidence are often by then compromised. Either way, these detectives know that solving their case relies heavily on their quickness to respond to the conflict immediately after it happens. The same should apply to you when resolving your conflicts.

Another challenge with taking a break or a time-out is that it is not always convenient or feasible. For example, an argument that happens inside of a car during a long road trip or during a group project with a stiff deadline might be challenging to walk away from. Sure, you could walk away in your mind, but would that be the productive thing to do at that point? Probably not. Besides, it would make the situation incredibly awkward and uncomfortable.

These examples make it much harder to just walk away and take a break or time-out. In fact, the term *"break"* is not even necessarily an accurate term for what we are really trying to communicate. The word *"break"* means to separate into pieces as a result of a blow, shock, or strain. It means to shatter, smash, crack, snap, fracture, fragment, splinter, or fall to pieces. Most of those descriptions would cause us to stop indefinitely, more or less take a break. They would require us to take a significant amount of time away, much less a time-out.

Again, if a time-out or break is for a brief moment, then it can be effective. A well-executed time-out or break during a crisis can be a lifesaver. Just ask any sports coaches who call time-outs when their opponents start to get in rhythm and make a run against their teams. Interrupting that momentum can be a good thing. In fact, taking time to pause is essentially like taking a break or time-out. However, anything beyond a short break or time-out that is not resolved the same day or within that moment falls into the danger zone.

The Apostle Paul wrote in Ephesians 4:26-27 (NLT), "And don't sin by letting anger control you. Don't let the sun go down while you are still angry, for anger gives a foothold to the devil." We are not supposed to let anger, resentment, or frustration linger around till the next day. Paul says we should make the attempt to resolve it that same day. Also, noticed Paul says we sin by letting anger control us. God wants us to nip anger in the bud immediately. He does not want us harboring anger, frustration, or any other inner anxiety. God knows that anger or inner anxiety is not one of the normal modes of life. It is a mode often used by the enemy to derail us.

Time-outs or breaks works well for children up to age six. In fact, many clinical studies have supported that notion. However, we are not children anymore who do not know how to handle our emotions correctly. We don't need a time-out or a break every time we experience a severe conflict. Usually, the problem is with our pride. Our pride gets in the way, and we refuse to admit that we are wrong or even consider that we might be wrong. Besides, all the extended time-outs and breaks that typically last for days, weeks, and even months do is give us time to finally come to the obvious conclusion that we were wrong or should have apologized in the first place. What a waste of time!

The Case for P.A.U.S.E.

Again, the challenge with taking a time-out or break is that usually, when they are suggested, it is well after the conflict has already ensued and is at its tipping point. Activating the P.A.U.S.E. mode is about trying your best to be diligent enough to identify and prevent conflicts before they actually happen. This can be a tough task if one is not diligent or walking prayerfully.

The good news is, if one forgets to enable the P.A.U.S.E. mode prior to a conflict, one can simply enable it wherever they are in that same conflict and work themselves out of that very issue. We'll discuss this point more in Chapter 9, titled, *"Mastering the Art of the P.A.U.S.E."*

The word *"pause"* represents a brief interruption, breathing space, hesitation, thinking carefully, or reflection. The P.A.U.S.E. mode is the antidote to the stop mode. The truth remains, in life, we don't always have the luxury of stopping until we figure things out. Effectively utilizing the P.A.U.S.E. mode enables us to stay in the play mode while we briefly walk through the steps of P.A.U.S.E. in order to resolve the conflict at hand, and then get back to play. Rather than ceasing all activity when conflict arises, one can simply take time to pause or rather P.A.U.S.E. The P.A.U.S.E. mode is a place for self-reflection. It is a place where one can quickly assess their current mental, emotional, and spiritual state, and then make a quick adjustment. It is a place where one can initiate a brief interruption to pause, gather their thoughts and then walk through the steps of P.A.U.S.E. to resolve any conflict that comes their way.

The P.A.U.S.E. mode is not for the weak or faint of heart. It is much easier to get into the stop mode than it is to get into the P.A.U.S.E. Quitting is always easier than winning. Walking away is always easier than sticking it out or seeing things through. When frustration sets in during conflict, tension will typically increase. However, God's design for us is to persevere. He said that we are more than overcomers. We are the ones who apparently have not read that memo. It is through our perseverance that our true character is defined and born.

Paul said in Romans 5:3-4 (NKJV), "And not only that but we also glory in tribulations, knowing that tribulation produces perseverance; and perseverance, character; and character, hope." Activating the P.A.U.S.E. mode is all about persevering through any conflict and any obstacle that comes your way. The next time you find yourself in a conflict, instead of reacting immediately to the situation, take time to instead respond through the steps of P.A.U.S.E. (Probe, Ask, Unlock, Suggest, and Evaluate) in a calm, cool, and collected manner. Walking through these steps effectively is a sure way to quickly resolve any conflict in your life and get your life back into the play mode where you belong. Over the next five chapters, we'll go into great detail about each acronym of the P.A.U.S.E. mode, show you the Biblical principles it was founded on, and then teach you how to apply them to your everyday communicative situations. These five steps will help you immensely as long as you embrace them with an open heart and mind. Are you ready? If so, let's embark on this life-changing journey!

Chapter 4

P = Probe

"Be anxious for nothing, but in everything by prayer..."

The word *"probe"* means to explore, examine, check, poke or feel around. It means to investigate, study, research, seek to uncover, or dissect. In middle or high school biology class, students will usually at some point dissect a frog. There are many reasons why students are asked to perform these dissections. The main purpose is to enable them to better understand the frog's body, so they will, in return, better understand their own bodies. Even though the functions of a frog and human body are very different, there are still organs present within the frog that correlate with the human body. The frog and the human are two completely different species; however, the students are still able to find a few common denominators between the two.

Humans, though slightly different, are all very similar as well. For the most part, we all have a head, a body, arms, and legs. Though different shades of color, we all still have similar facial features and the same type of internal organs functioning within ourselves. Some of us have very similar, and some of us, very different personalities. When we take the time to dissect someone's personality that is much different from ours, it can feel much like dissecting a frog. We will see slight similarities between them and ourselves. However, we will usually clearly identify that we are completely different people. We all have our own little idiosyncrasies that we prefer. We all have our own way of doing things that present a certain level of comfort in our lives. These routine habits often make us feel safe and secure. They often help us mitigate the element of surprise that life can frequently present to us in this world.

When one chooses to probe, they choose to make themselves a bit uncomfortable. Their train of thought is not focused merely on themselves but the security and safety of others. Probing is a selfless act that requires one to examine others for spiritual wounds and emotional setbacks. It is not an act of only examining one's outward appearance, but of utilizing spiritual discernment to examine the condition of one's soul.

When we probe effectively, we dissect and assess every situation that we encounter. Rather than being quick to pass judgment, one who probes will instead carefully analyze a situation to determine the correct course of action. They will methodically dissect the facts and place them in order to study the parts for truth. They are probing to gain more clarity and insight, not to overly scrutinize one's performance or behavior. They are not probing to bring justice; they are probing to understand.

Walking Prayerfully

The word *"probe"* also means to walk prayerfully. Walking prayerfully means walking consciously and intentionally with God. When one walks with God, they walk with love. In fact, everything they probe should be seen through a lens of love. When one effectively probes, they seek to understand the situation, first knowing that this method will enable them to make a sound decision later. Someone who probes well, listens well. Their spiritual ears are open to hear the cry for help from one's soul. They are also incredibly great at watching and gathering information from others. They would often make great hunters.

Lions, tigers, wolves, and bears are all great hunters. One of the biggest keys to their success is their patience. Great hunters understand that reacting too fast can cost them a good meal. Their ability to wait and properly assess the situation gives them a huge advantage. Great hunters also realize that they ought to have respect for their prey. Even though they desire to conquer their prey, they still understand that if they fail to respect the skills and qualities of their prey, it could cost them dearly. In some cases, it could even cost them their own lives. Using any kind of bait for their prey does not work. A great hunter probes by studying what their prey likes and dislikes, and then prepares accordingly. They always have their weapons and are well prepared to hunt.

Much like a hunter, we should make it a point to study each other. We obviously shouldn't study to take advantage of or kill each other; instead, we should, with the intent that we ourselves will benefit from what we learn about others. How much conflict would we avoid if we took more time to understand each other? What would the outcome look like if we took the time to prayerfully assess a situation rather than overreacting when someone was rude to us? Sometimes we fight fire with fire, yet we wonder why we end up burnt. Great probers are great spiritual hunters who look for opportunities to encourage and strengthen one's spirit. They don't hide from conflict; they run toward conflict because they know they have the solution. They have the P.A.U.S.E. mode.

Walking prayerfully means having the awareness to identify and admit that a problem exists. It doesn't do us much good to probe and keep overlooking obvious problems. A problem that is not first identified cannot be later corrected or healed. We often struggle with this revelation when we probe ourselves. It is tough to admit that you are the problem or have a problem. Admitting that you have a problem is not a negative confession, it is a self-confession or self-diagnosis. It is you admitting to yourself and acknowledging the fact that you need help. We cannot get well if we do not know how to ask for help.

For example, if one is sick and goes to the doctor, the doctor may ask, "What is bothering you?" If that person replies to the doctor, stating that nothing is wrong, will that person be healed? Of course not! Once the patient is honest enough to expresses to the doctor what is ailing them, the doctor can then effectively *"probe"* the situation and remedy the issue.

We love to encourage ourselves, yet, we don't love to probe ourselves. The Apostle Paul said in 2 Corinthians 13:5 (NIV), "Examine yourselves to see whether you are in the faith; test yourselves." Are you battle tested? Are you constantly probing yourself to make sure that there are no ill feelings within you? Sometimes when we probe, we will find that the problem was us from the very beginning.

Many people isolate themselves when they have issues, making it tough for someone else to probe their situation and help. Somewhere along the line, we have learned that it is a negative confession to say I have a headache, I'm in pain, or I feel like a loser, and so we stop expressing ourselves. The problem is not in the confession; the lack of knowing what to do after we confess our problem is the issue. One cannot remedy a problem without first acknowledging that they have a problem. In these situations, it is easy to allow our pride and feelings to get in the way of true healing.

A feeling is an emotional state or reaction to a particular situation. We all have feelings and can have those very feelings hurt, whether we want to admit it or not. In fact, anyone who tells you that they don't have feelings is just expressing to you how they feel. God programmed us to have feelings. Without feelings, it would be difficult to express love. Asking someone why they are emotional or why they are in their feelings is like asking someone why they are human. God created us to have feelings, and He loves us just the way we are; you should too.

We get ourselves in trouble when we let our feelings primarily guide us in our decision-making. Our feelings and emotions are part of our subconscious mind. The probe step is done through our conscious mind. Our life experiences that we encounter in the conscious mind create the emotions and feelings that dwell within our subconscious mind. If we are always around negative, argumentative, complaining people in our conscious mind, those experiences will then produce negative, argumentative, complaining feelings and emotions in our subconscious mind. That is why watching negative TV shows or listening to derogatory music is a bad idea. When your conscious mind experiences these events, it has no other choice but to produce and send corresponding emotions and feelings down to your subconscious.

Our subconscious mind does not control when our emotions and feelings are expressed. Our subconscious mind only acts as a storage room for our feelings and emotions and releases those emotions when it believes their release is necessary. It is our conscious mind that controls and filters our emotions and feelings. When we fail to probe or examine ourselves, we fail to use our conscious mind. That is why so many people will express words without a filter or say or do something that they would later regret. They are not operating within their conscious mind. They are instead being guided by their feelings and emotions within their subconscious mind.

The Apostle Peter used to be a hot-tempered, unfiltered person; however, you can see his growth and maturity in 1 Peter 5:8 (NIV) when he said, "Be alert and of sober mind. Your enemy, the devil, prowls around like a roaring lion looking for someone to devour." Sober doesn't just mean not to be drunk; sober means to be levelheaded. It means to be practical, sensible, realistic, and rational. It means to not be overly emotional. Our feelings and emotions are fine, as long as we filter them and don't allow them to control us. When we act on only what we feel and remove logic from the equation, we are not being sober-minded. We're acting in a way that is equivalent to someone who is drunk. I don't know about you, but if I'm going to be under the influence, I'd rather be under the influence of the Holy Spirit than my own feelings and emotions.

Walking prayerfully allows one to effectively probe in the Spirit and not in our feelings. Probe means constantly checking the inner temperature gauge in our minds for signs of anxiety. It involves knowing the conflict warning signs of both yourself and others with whom you communicate. Signs like sweating palms, a sweating forehead, a face turning red, a lack of eye contact, deep breaths, an unusual quietness, a rising tone, gritting teeth, shaky legs or hands, biting on the bottom lip, or tapping of the feet are all signs or symptoms of potential conflict. When we ignore these warning signs, we are failing to probe. When we effectively use the probe step, we will make it a point to figure out what is bothering us or the other party involved. We will prayerfully identify and acknowledge the issue, or if not yet located, pursue it until we have found it.

Probe Intentionally Pursues

Probing is offensively-minded, not defensively-minded or reactive. When you probe, you intentionally pursue and initiate. You don't just react to an outcome; you strategically respond. Just as love pursues, probe pursues. When we are probing others prayerfully, and in a loving way, we are acting like Christ. We are showing others the love of God. David wrote in Psalms 139:4-7 (NIV), "Before a word is on my tongue you, Lord, know it completely. You hem me in behind and before, and you lay your hand upon me. Such knowledge is too wonderful for me, too lofty for me to attain. Where can I go from your Spirit? Where can I flee from your presence?" David wasn't making a complaint to God about Him stalking him. David was amazed and overwhelmed at how much God paid attention to him. Are the people you know amazed at how much you pay attention to them? Are they amazed by how well you listen to them? Are they overwhelmed by how loving you are towards them? Are you probing to bless or to curse? Don't answer that just yet. Let's first go a little deeper to find out what it truly means when we probe to bless.

Probe to Bless, Not Curse

We empower others to reach their destinies when we effectively probe. Probing allows us the ability to identify areas where we can be a blessing to someone else. When we choose to be a blessing to others, God, in return, helps us reach our own destinies. It is better known as the law of giving and receiving. We live in a time where it is so easy to become selfish or self-absorbed. Sure, life can be incredibly difficult and present us with daily challenges. However, taking our focus off of probing can open the door again for inner anxiety to creep back into our lives. We must continually examine ourselves and others.

Have you ever felt irritated out of nowhere and couldn't figure out why? Have you ever awakened in the morning in a bad mood for no rhyme or reason? The slightest situation in our lives that goes wrong will set us off quickly if we fail to walk prayerfully. If we fail to consistently probe ourselves and others, we will fail in our relationships.

Usually, when we fail to probe, inner anxiety takes up its home again and starts to produce stress, anger, frustration, envy, jealousy, and fear. Over time, the lens we use to probe can become dirty if we fail to examine ourselves. Instead of probing out of love, we can then probe out of excessive scrutiny. For example, our spouse or children may say or do something annoying that gets under our skin. Instead of responding through a lens of love, we will respond with a dirty lens filled with complaints, frustration or anger. Or perhaps, a co-worker at work becomes jealous of us, and instead of them showing us love, they spread untrue facts about us. As a result, we may respond in an unloving way to correct them by verbally ripping them apart. Now, I know you don't have this problem, but believe me, it happens. It is a dangerous state of mind.

Probing is dangerous when it is used to bring judgment on someone or something. We were not created to judge or dominate each other; Christ is our judge and our king. We were created to bless and to be a blessing. We should probe only to bless, not to curse. We should probe to bring healing and edification, not to hurt and tear down. The probe step is meant to help us identify an issue quickly, so we can resolve it through love. Many issues are resolved by one simply choosing to cover the fault rather than exposing it or pointing it out to the offender.

We should probe to heal or cover faults, not expose them. Not every fault we identify through probing needs to be publicly expressed or condemned openly. In fact, Jesus expressed the idea that if our brother or sister sins, we should point it out with them privately and if they listen, we have won them over. People don't like to be exposed or made to look silly or dumb. When we say things that publicly embarrass someone, we are failing to probe and walk prayerfully. We are not walking in love.

The Bible also shares a story about Jesus in John Chapter 8 when a woman and man were caught in the act of adultery. The teachers of the law and Pharisees of that time brought the woman to Jesus, reminding Him that such a woman should be stoned to death according to the Law of Moses. In that moment, Jesus could have reacted quickly and said: "Stone her!" He could have verbally scolded her and cursed her. However, instead, Jesus probed the situation. He knelt down and started to write on the ground with his finger. Now, the Bible doesn't tell us what Jesus wrote. Still, I think it is interesting that it does tell us that he wrote with His finger on the ground as if He did not hear them speaking to Him. Jesus intentionally blocked out all of the white noise.

Usually, when we write in the dirt with our fingers, we typically use our index finger; the same finger we often use to point out something. Perhaps Jesus was illustrating to the teachers of the law and Pharisees just how dirty their pointed fingers were. Perhaps He was showing them how sinful and flawed they were as they pointed their fingers at the adulterous woman. I say this because Jesus responded and said to them, "Let any one of you who is without sin be the first to throw a stone at her." The Bible goes on to say that all who heard this statement began to walk away one at a time until only Jesus and the woman were left standing there. Jesus then asked her, "Woman, where are they? Has no one condemned you?" "No one, sir," she replied. "Then neither do I condemn you, go now and leave your life of sin." Jesus declared. What is also interesting is the fact that Jesus practiced what He preached by waiting to confront the woman about her sin privately instead of publicly. He waited until everyone had left and it was just the two of them. I'm sure she appreciated that, and I'm sure Jesus won her over that day!

Use the probe step to identify problems quickly. Pay attention to the signs. The faster you identify them, the faster you can work through the remaining steps to resolve them. When conflict arises in the play mode of life, our first instinct should be to halt and go into the P.A.U.S.E. mode so we can utilize the probe step. The faster we probe, the faster we can work through the remaining steps and get back to living our best life in the play mode.

Chapter 5

$A = Ask$

"...and supplication..."

The battle of the mind is a very real struggle that we all have to encounter on a daily basis. Having the resolve to fight off negative thoughts and feelings is much easier said than done. Our minds are constantly bombarded with thoughts that are both positive and negative. However, it is up to us to ultimately decide which thoughts leave our minds and which remains.

A desire is a strong feeling or a want to possess something. It is a strong wish we have for something we would like to see happen. It is something we long for, yearn for, or crave. When we have a strong desire for something, we are typically in a place where we have to ask for it. If that were not the case, we would simply obtain what we desire. There would be no need for the desire to increase to the point of a "strong desire."

The Bible says in James 4:1-3 (NIV), "What causes fights and quarrels among you? Don't they come from your desires that battle within you? You desire but do not have, so you kill. You covet but you cannot get what you want, so you quarrel and fight. You do not have because you do not ask God. When you ask, you do not receive, because you ask with wrong motives, that you may spend what you get on your pleasures."

We may not have physically killed someone; however, how many relationships have we killed due to our own personal desires? How many arguments or fights have you been involved in because you didn't get your own way? You may be perfect and have never had this issue. However, the rest of us will admit that there have been times where we have allowed our own desires to cause conflict. Our own battles within ourselves have caused us to fight or argue with someone because we both desired different things.

Having a desire for or coveting something is not necessarily a bad thing, as long as the thing we desire or covet is in line with God's will. Paul has been quoted in the Bible, telling us to covet certain spiritual gifts. Also, the Bible says that if we delight ourselves in the Lord, He will give us the desires of our heart. That doesn't mean He will give us what we want; it means He will download

His desires for our lives inside of us. From there, they will formulate and manifest as our very own desires. For example, have you ever had a desire out of nowhere to help someone else? Have you ever had a desire inside of you to accomplish something great that would benefit others? Desires like these come from our Heavenly Father as every good and perfect gift comes from Him.

Hurting People, Hurt People

Oftentimes, when we are disappointed or frustrated with others, we are disappointed and frustrated with our own outcome in life. Some of us may have thought that we would have been further along in life by now educationally, financially, or spiritually. We see so many others moving along in life, and we ask ourselves, "Why not me?" The pain, hurt, and frustration we experience through our own disappointments can often spill into our relationships and affect how we treat others. If our lives are great, we will treat others great. If our lives are bad, others would be wise to avoid us at all costs.

Paul said in 1 Corinthians 14:1 (NIV), "Follow the way of love and eagerly desire gifts of the Spirit, especially prophecy." Notice first that Paul said to follow the way of love. God is love, so Paul is simply saying follow the ways of God. Secondly, Paul says eagerly desire the gifts of the Spirit. Notice he did not say to desire material things; he said to desire the gifts of the Spirit. Putting a strong emphasis on material things often leads to jealousy, fights, or to our own disappointment. Putting a strong emphasis on spiritual things gives us a strong sense of meaning and purpose. That is usually due to the fact that when we focus on spiritual things, we will eventually identify our spiritual gifts.

All of us are given at least one spiritual gift from the Holy Spirit (1 Cor. 12:11). However, notice also in the scripture above that Paul says to especially desire prophecy. Why is that gift so important? Why does Paul specifically point this gift out? Prophecy is simply foretelling the future. When we prophesy over our lives, we foretell what our future will become. The spiritual realm responds to the commands of our prophecies. Just as God spoke the world into existence, we can create our own world with our words. We are made in His image and given that same power as we speak through the Word of God.

So then, if we have such great power as this, why are we so often frustrated with life? Could the problem possibly be that we are upset about not having something that God never intended us to have in the first place?

Could the problem be that your negativity or argumentative attitude is keeping away the very people God desires to use to bless you? Could the fact that you are not walking in unity with God and them be the reason that your prayers are not answered? Sometimes, it is our own disobedience and reluctance to follow God's plan that makes us miserable. That is why Paul said above that "You covet but you cannot get what you want, so you quarrel and fight."

There is power in united supplication. There is power when we touch and agree with each other and then ask God to come through for us, according to His will. There are no lone rangers in the kingdom of God. God loves and honors unity. That is why Jesus said in Matthew 18:19 (NIV), "Again, truly I tell you that if two of you on earth agree about anything they ask for, it will be done for them by my Father in heaven." We can make bad decisions on our own. However, it is usually more difficult to get someone else to go along with our dumb ideas. Usually, someone will at some point say that we are out of our minds to think or do that. Have you ever noticed how easy it is to counsel someone else about their problems while we struggle to figure out our own? Being in a relationship with someone allows them to see our blind spots and touch and agree once we discover God's will for our lives.

Many times, it is our own lack of spiritual and emotional maturity that holds us back from accomplishing our desires. Notice in the last part of the above scripture Paul states, "When you ask, you do not receive, because you ask with wrong motives, that you may spend what you get on your pleasures." God wants to give us what He wants for our lives, not what we alone want for our lives. Everything He wants for our lives is good and will always prosper us. Everything we want for our lives is not always good and does not always prosper us.

When our desires in life are not met, we eventually can become hurt. *Hurting people, hurt people.* When we probe ourselves and find that we feel angry, bitter, resentful, or frustrated, a great practice is to ask ourselves, "Why do I feel this way?" When we probe and notice that others with whom we have a relationship are bothered, we should also ask them why they are bothered. It is important that we ask these questions so that we can identify the issue. Identifying an issue and then asking the right questions about that issue allows us to better understand the issue at hand.

Ask to Identify

The word, "supplication" means the action of asking or begging for something earnestly or humbly. It means to plea, petition, request, or ask prayerfully. When we find ourselves in the middle of a conflict, after we *Probe*, we should then *Ask*. After we go into the P.A.U.S.E. mode and probe the situation, we should then ask as many questions necessary in order to gain a clear understanding. Without first identifying the problem, one cannot move on with the remaining steps of the P.A.U.S.E. mode. Notice I said identifying the problem and not identifying what's wrong with someone. It may sound like the same thing, but it's not.

Most people mean well in life and do not desire to be mean, frustrated or stressed. More often than not, there is something that is bothering them or affecting them negatively, which, in return, influences them to act negatively or feel a way that is inconsistent with their normal mode of life. Asking someone, "What's wrong with you?" in oppose to "What's wrong?" or "What's bothering you?" may not seem like a big deal, however, trust me, it is. Asking someone "What is bothering you?" in oppose to asking, "Why are you so bothered?" can deescalate or escalate an issue quickly.

Remember, we should desire the way of love when it comes to asking. If our asking is wrapped in love, we will not pose a threat to someone else. If our asking is not wrapped in love, one might become defensive.

However, love is not always the issue. Sometimes, when asking a question to identify a problem, one might be reluctant to express what is ailing them. Maybe they are afraid to be vulnerable or too upset to express how they feel. Nevertheless, when we ask with humility and through love, we create an environment that feels safe and conducive to their transparency. A safe environment always makes us feel comfortable. Inner anxiety hates safe environments; it thrives and feeds off of stressful and fearful environments.

Asking to identify is about taking the warning signs you discover in the probe step and comparing your findings with the symptoms someone verbally expresses when you ask questions. For example, when a sick patient visits the doctor's office, the doctor will examine (or probe) the patient for any visual warning signs. The doctor may check their eyes, ears, mouth, arms, legs, or even their heart pulse. Once the doctor finishes this procedure, he will then often ask the patient how they feel. If he is a good doctor, he won't ask a lot of questions without probing first. He may ask the patient a question or two. However, his primary concern is to first take a look at the patient to see what he identifies. Once he has ruled out other sicknesses, he will then usually ask the patient a few specific questions to identify the sickness. Even though the doctor may have already identified or formed a guess as to what the sickness might be, he will still ask some clarifying questions just to be sure. He is not asking in order to justify how smart he is to the patient; he is asking to understand.

Ask to Understand

Asking should be done in a non-defensive way. One should ask questions humbly in order to gain more facts. They should ask earnestly and seek to understand, not to be understood or to justify themselves. Understanding something means to interpret or view it in a particular way. It means to make the thing we are trying to understand more clear. It means to make something more plain or shed light on it. The light is not meant to expose the thing we are viewing; it is used to examine, identify, and understand the very thing we are viewing.

When we seek to understand the symptoms and the causes of a problem, we move closer to the healing process and finding antidotes to prevent the problem from reoccurring. As long as we are predominantly concerned with being heard, justified, or right, we will struggle to resolve conflicts. Moving towards resolving conflict in the ask step is about asking to understand the other person's point of view, not asking to justify ourselves.

Most of us are able to properly probe, identify, and even ask the right questions when we notice that someone is upset about a particular matter. The place where most of us go wrong is when someone has an issue with something we may have said or done. The truth is, when you love someone, you will defend that person even when that person might have been wrong. Fans always defend their teams win, lose, or draw. We love and are fans of ourselves; therefore, it is often difficult for us to become critical of ourselves. We have a hard time distinguishing between constructive criticism and negative criticism when it comes to ourselves. However, we have no issue criticizing others when they are wrong or offend us.

Jesus knew this all along, which is why He only gave us two commandments to fulfill in Matthew 22:37-39 (NIV) when he said "Love the Lord your God with all your heart and with all your soul and with all your mind. This is the first and greatest commandment. And the second is like it: Love your neighbor as yourself." Jesus knows that if we love God, we will love His people. Also, if we love our neighbor as we love ourselves, we will treat our neighbor like we treat ourselves. We will love them unconditionally the same way we love ourselves. However, for some reason, we struggle to do just that.

Look, I understand that the ask step can be an extremely difficult step. Sometimes we may have done nothing wrong. Perhaps the other person was wrong, mean, unloving, or disrespectful. Even with that, the same rules apply; that is what loving unconditionally is all about. We should still ask to understand why the other person is upset with us and not justify why we believe we are right. That is why Jesus said to bless those who curse us and to pray for those who take advantage of us. It is easy to love those that love us. The real challenge is loving and treating others better than ourselves when they don't deserve that love. The ask step is for the spiritually mature, not the faint of heart.

Ask What One Desires

I know what you're thinking. You think if you don't justify yourself, you will appear weak, passive, ignorant, or lose the upper hand. Well, let me ask you this; Jesus never justified Himself when He was crucified, and did He lose the upper hand? Is He not King of Kings and Lord of Lords? Will not every head bow and tongue confess that

He is Lord? Jesus could have easily pleaded His case to Pilate for His innocence. He could have easily defended His life. However, He chose to lay His life down despite knowing that He did nothing wrong. Why is that an issue for us?

Jesus chose to lay His life down to save us. Why wouldn't you lay your life down to save your relationship? Don't let your pride trick you into thinking that you refusing to justify yourself means you are weak, a pushover, and will be taken advantage of by your accusers. There is incredible strength and power in someone who is innocent yet chooses to lay down their life or their desire to be right in order to save their neighbor, their spouse, or the person they love. Supplication also means to pray and ask God. We should always seek God through prayer and ask the Holy Spirit to guide us through our questioning process when it comes to conflict resolution. Merely relying on our own reasoning is a recipe for disaster.

When we ask, we are asking to identify and understand what one desires. A great waiter or waitress at a restaurant is great at asking questions. In fact, some of the world's top waiters and waitresses that provide excellent service and produce their businesses the highest revenues ask the most questions. These servers understand that they are present to do just that, serve. They will ask if you have any questions about the menu, ask if you would like to start off with an appetizer, ask what you would like to drink, or if you would like to upsize or add an additional item. They realize that the more they identify and understand what you desire, the more options they can present you from their menu. This approach is also what leads to great customer experiences.

Customers like to be listened to and love for their considerations to be acknowledged. It is no different when it comes to our relationships. People who we do life together with want to be heard, understood and acknowledged. In fact, the servers that are great at making their customers feel like they are present and very attentive usually receive the bigger tips as their reward.

If you want to exemplify the love and power of Christ in your life, choose to serve rather than always being served. Become okay with being viewed as wrong even though you know deep down that you are right. Resist the urge to keep justifying yourself. Love God with all of your heart and love others like you love yourself. When we ask what one desires out of love, we diffuse their anger, frustration, or bitterness. We find out what is truly the issue, rather than influencing them to become defensive because we keep trying to justify ourselves.

John 15:13 (NIV) says, "Greater love has no one than this: to lay down one's life for one's friends." Don't be afraid to lay down your defense. Stop fighting battles that God wants you to surrender to. Surrender in God's kingdom is not losing; surrender in His kingdom is winning. This world doesn't understand that concept. When we ask with humility, sincerity, and through a loving heart, we will uncover where the real issue lies. Sometimes, one might be mad at us for one thing. However, after asking questions and digging deeper, we will discover that the current issue was just a trigger. There was actually a bigger and deeper issue at hand.

Stop justifying yourself, and let God justify you. If someone is wrong, your job is not to prove that they are wrong. Your job is to make sure you are not wrong. When we make sure that we are not wrong, we allow God to do a work that only He can do inside of the life of the other person. Stop fighting and pleading your case, and you will unlock doors that you had never dreamt would open. Take time to probe and then ask questions to identify, to understand, and to find out what one desires. Do this well enough, and you will be on your way to resolving any conflicts that you experience in your relationships.

Chapter 6

U = Unlock

"...with thanksgiving..."

A heart of humility, gratitude, and thankfulness grants access to a hardened, prideful, and unforgiving heart. When one executes the *"Probe"* and *"Ask"* steps effectively, they will seamlessly transition into the *"Unlock"* step. When we humbly ask questions to understand why we or someone else is upset, we gather the necessary information to transition ourselves or others into the unlock step. When we ask questions in a defensive way or ask questions to respond with our justification for our actions, we lock our hearts and the hearts of others.

Unlock means to open up, let loose, undo, or make known what was previously unknown. It means to unbolt, unlatch, unseal, unclose, or make accessible. The unlock step is about restoration and reconciliation through thanksgiving. When we ask our questions with thanksgiving, we diffuse the ticking time bomb inside of one's head that is waiting to explode with anger, rage, or frustration. We unlock love which counters fear, anger, doubt, or any other inner anxieties one may be experiencing.

The unlock step is where healing takes place. It is a place where it is perfectly safe to be open and vulnerable. It is not a place of judgment; it is a place of grace. It is not a place of condemnation; it is a place of approval and praise. It is a place where appreciation, gratitude and love are openly expressed. It is not a prideful place; it is a place for the spiritually and emotionally mature. Pride locks the heart while love unlocks it. When a heart becomes prideful, it becomes closed and locked up. A locked-up heart eventually becomes hardened, and a hardened heart becomes desensitized.

The Hardened Heart

The dictionary defines hardened as cold, insensitive, unfeeling, unyielding, or desensitized. A hardened heart is thickened, toughened, or fortress-like. A fortress is often described as a military stronghold such as a fort, castle, bunker, or tower. However, a fortress is also a person that is not susceptible to outside influences or disturbances.

Our hearts are not meant to be fortified. Sure, our physical hearts are fortified inside of our bodies, of course, for protection. However, the heart in itself is not fortified within the body. It serves as the distributor of our blood within our bodies. The heart fills itself up with blood and then pumps the blood to the right and left ventricles. The ventricles then contract together and pump the blood out of the heart.

The same is true for our spiritual hearts. When we confess Jesus Christ as our Lord, we become part of the body of Christ. We then share the same blood as siblings and as children of God. Our bloodline becomes one of Royalty. Our hearts must remain completely open and free for the blood of Christ to flow through them. Our hearts must remain free and open to pump out the love of Christ to all whom we meet and encounter. A heart that does not flow becomes a dried-up heart; a dried-up heart becomes a hardened heart.

God enables our hearts to be hardened so we can shut out unwanted influences. However, once again, the devil has found a way to distort God's intentions by convincing us to harden our hearts during the wrong circumstances. A hardened heart dries up our ability to clearly perceive and understand. This is why so many people struggle to relate to or connect with God. They have a hardened heart towards Him. Their faith in Him has dried up.

Jesus experienced the same hardness of heart with His own disciples. Mark 8:17 (NKJV) says, "But Jesus being aware of it, said to them, 'Why do you reason because you have no bread? Do you not yet perceive nor understand? Is your heart still hardened? Having eyes, do you not see? And having ears, do you not hear? And do you not remember? When I broke the five loaves for the five thousand, how many baskets full of fragments did you take up?" Jesus had just finished performing a miracle in front of the disciples when He fed well over five thousand people by miraculously multiplying loaves of bread and fish. Nevertheless, His disciples still struggled with their faith in Christ. They continued to be shocked and amazed at His miracles, instead of having complete trust that Jesus could do anything.

Our relationships become strained and stale when we lose our faith in them. When we fail to trust God or those who we are in relationship with, we distort our perception and understanding of them. Jesus gave us three signs above of a hardened heart. He stated that a hardened heart does not see, hear, or remember. When we fail to see the work that God is doing in our lives; when we fail to hear His voice comforting and guiding us; when we fail to remember the miracles He has already performed in our lives, our hearts will become hardened. Similarly, when we fail to see our relationships with others through the correct lens; when we fail to listen to them with an understanding ear; when we fail to remember the good they have done for us, our hearts become hardened!

When our hearts are hardened, we become spiritually blind and deaf. We fail to see the revelations in scripture or clearly hear the sermons at church. We fail to adequately express our emotions or sympathy toward others. We become desensitized to the world around us. When our hearts are hardened, we become a risk and threat to others. Because we are unable to see, hear, or remember correctly, we will often misconstrue the words of others or become unthankful for their past good deeds. When this happens, we often unintentionally offend them, even though in our minds, we did not mean any offense.

Where We Go Wrong

A hardened heart almost always leads to an unintentional offense. Where we go wrong is when we refuse to quickly apologize after an offense. Our refusal to quickly apologize often causes the person whom we offended to resent us even more. Instead of reconciling, our focus then centers on justifying our actions. Our primary focus then becomes self-preservation; we are focused on solely being right, even at the expense of an argument.

Viewing or remembering the offense as only one way is also where we go wrong. When we are sure that the other person is wrong and fail to examine ourselves in the process, we have a hardened heart. A sign that we do not have a hardened heart is when we are willing to consider the possibility that we might be wrong even when we know for a fact that we are right. We should always be willing to probe ourselves. Whether we are right or wrong is not really the main concern. The main concern is in the conflict in itself, which creates division and ultimately separates us from one another. The devil doesn't care which one of us is right or wrong; he just wants us to fight.

Jesus understood this truth and was well aware of the devil's methods, which is why he said in Matthew 5:23-24 (NKJV), "Therefore if you bring your gift to the altar, and there remember that your brother has something against you, leave your gift there before the altar, and go your way. First, be reconciled to your brother, and then come and offer your gift." What was Jesus saying here? Notice Jesus used the word "remember" and not the word "discover."

Remember means to bring to one's mind an awareness of someone or something that one has seen, known, or experienced in the past. In other words, Jesus said if you remember the offense, that means you acknowledge it was previously there. You can't remember what you have never known. In other words, Jesus was saying that you didn't just now discover that you offended that person; you already knew that person was offended. Jesus commands us to resolve and make the matter right before we receive our blessing. So many people are withholding their own blessings from God because they refuse to resolve an offense.

Jesus also said in the same passage of scripture, "Therefore if you bring your gift to the altar, and there remember..." Bringing a gift to the altar is symbolic for worship. It is amazing how things are revealed to us when we start to worship God. When we worship God, He will show us ourselves in the past, present and future. He will reveal the good, the bad, and the ugly. He doesn't do it to expose us; He does it because He loves us. He wants us to be free to move forward in life without anything holding us back. He wants us to be fully restored back to the image He has of us. He wants us to worship without guilt or shame, which is why the Bible also says in John 4:24 (NKJV), "God is Spirit, and those who worship Him must worship in spirit and truth." You may be wondering, "What if the offended person is being overly sensitive to my actions or remarks? What if I am communicating or acting through love; however, they are receiving it wrong due to their hardened heart?" I'm glad you asked! In order to find that answer, let's look back at the scriptures.

Notice Jesus starts Matthew 5:23 (NKJV) off with the word, "Therefore." Whenever the word "Therefore" is present, it impels us to look back before the word to discover what it is in fact "there for." In this case, look at what Matthew 5:21-22 says, "You have heard that it was said to those of old, 'You shall not murder, and whoever murders will be in danger of the judgment.' But I say to you that whoever is angry with his brother without a cause shall be in danger of the judgment. And whoever says to his brother, 'Raca!' shall be in danger of the council. But whoever says, 'You fool!' shall be in danger of hell fire."

Jesus addresses the overly sensitive person in the previous verses prior to giving us the command to leave our gifts at the altar. Look again at what He says, "But I say to you that whoever is angry with his brother *without a cause...*" If someone is being overly sensitive or misinterpreting what you said or did, they are angry without a cause. The fact of the matter is, if they are acting out of love and from a sincere heart, they would also use the

"Probe" and "Ask" steps. They would probe the situation and then ask additional questions to gain more clarity as to what you meant by your words or actions. They would also consider probing themselves to ensure that they are not overreacting in any way. They would then "unlock" what you were really trying to express.

Being overly sensitive or misinterpreting a situation often causes us to jump to conclusions that are not totally accurate. Usually, when this happens, we are solely letting our feelings in the subconscious mind drive our reactions, instead of viewing the situation from a reasonable standpoint in our conscious mind. In some cases, an overly sensitive person or a person who misinterprets a situation will react negatively to a situation, making the matter even worse. They often tend to respond with harsh words or even call their offenders bad names. However, Jesus also addressed this issue as well when he said in verse 22, "…And whoever says to his brother, 'Raca!' shall be in danger of the council. But whoever says, 'You fool!' shall be in danger of hell fire."

The word "raca" is original to the Greek manuscript; however, it is not a Greek word. The most common view of this word is a reference to the Aramaic word "reka," which means "empty one" or "empty-headed." Jesus condemns the person that is angry without a cause and then concedes to the below-the-belt tactic of name-calling. In fact, He says they are in danger of earthly and spiritual punishment through council or hellfire if they don't repent. Refusing to unlock ourselves and apologize, or refusing to forgive those that offend us, only keeps us in the stop mode of life. It keeps us from experiencing our best life that God has already designed. It keeps us from enjoying our lives predominately in the play mode of life.

Unlocking Ourselves Unlocks Others

When we are honest and open first, we create an environment for the person who is upset or offended to be open and honest about how they feel. We create an environment that is safe and conducive to their openness. A person who chooses to unlock themselves first during a conflict is a thermostat controlling the climate rather than a thermometer reacting to the current climate. They are intentional about unlocking themselves in order to quickly resolve the conflict.

For example, if I had a bad day at work and came home frustrated, I may not be in the most talkative mood. If my wife, Faith, was very playful and loud with me, I could become irritated with her and lash out due to my inner anxiety. Faith would then feel offended and hurt by my words. My actions would probably cause her to withdraw from me both physically and emotionally, making the situation even more awkward. Now, before I wrote this book, and before I learned how to activate the P.A.U.S.E. mode, that would have been the end of the night for us. She and I would have not spoken to each other the rest of the evening and would have been mad at each other for days or even weeks! What a waste of time!

However, now when a situation like this happens, I stop and activate the P.A.U.S.E. mode. I first *"Probe"* and recognize that she is visually upset and also identify my wrongdoings internally. Yes, I admit that I was wrong. I make it a point to humbly and sincerely *"Ask"* her to forgive me for my poor reaction. At this point, Faith might still be mad even though I apologized. That is why the unlock step is so important. If still upset, I would then unlock myself by explaining to her that she did nothing wrong and would open up about some of the things that happened to me at work. Sometimes, Faith may even open up about some hidden issues she had been struggling with as well. Her playfulness towards me may have been an attempt to gain my attention so that I could encourage her through my affirmation and love towards her. If this is done correctly, the conflict will be resolved, and Faith and I can get back to life in the play mode. Unlocking ourselves unlocks others.

When we are offended or hurt, one of the last things we desire to do is open up and talk or show our wounds. The wound is usually still too fresh, and the pain has yet to subside. We often ask ourselves questions like, "How could they do this to me?" or "What did I do to deserve this?" or "Why does this always happen to me?"

Perhaps your thought is, "Why forgive someone over and over when they really are not sorry, or they will just do it again?" If you have felt this way, you are not the first. In fact, the Apostle Peter felt this same way and asked Jesus about it himself in Matthew 18:21-22 (NKJV), "Then Peter came to Him and said, 'Lord how often shall my brother sin against me, and I forgive him? Up to seven times?' Jesus said to him, 'I do not say to you, up to seven times, but up to seventy times seven." Jesus did not literally mean 490 times. Jesus was illustrating to Peter that forgiveness is not about us allowing the other person to get away with whatever they want. Forgiveness benefits us, not just the offender. Jesus was explaining to Peter that he needs to forgive indefinitely for the benefit of himself.

Jesus understands that holding onto an offense wastes too much time and energy. In fact, you don't have to go far to understand that Jesus is not giving those a pass who keep offending us. In the same chapter of Matthew, Jesus addressed how to deal with a person that keeps offending you. Jesus says in Matthew 18:15-17, "Moreover, if your brother sins against you, go and tell him his fault between you and him alone. If he hears you, you have gained your brother. But if he will not hear, take with you one or two more, that 'by the mouth of two or three witnesses every word may be established.' And if he refuses to hear them, tell it to the church. But if he refuses even to hear the church, let him be to you like a heathen and a tax collector."

Wow, what a powerful statement. As you see above, Jesus does not excuse someone from continually offending you, bullying you, or taking advantage of you. If you cannot handle the matter yourself, ask friends to help you make your case. If friends can't help, call on the leaders of the church to help. If the offender will not listen to the leaders of the church, Jesus said then let them go. However, notice He does not say that you do not have to forgive them.

After Jesus told Peter to forgive seventy times seven, He explained a parable to Peter. Jesus went on to talk about a king that wanted to settle all of his accounts with his servants. When the king had begun to settle accounts, one of his servants was brought to him that owed the king a lot of money. The servant was unable to pay the debt, so the king commanded that the servant, his wife, and children, along with all his possessions be sold as a payment for the debt. However, the servant begged the king for mercy so much that the king was moved with compassion, released the servant, and forgave him for the entire debt. However, the servant went out and found one of his own servants that owed him money. When he found one, he laid hands on him, demanded that the servant pay him what he owed him, and threw him in prison until the debt was paid. The king found out what his servant did and was greatly upset. The king delivered the servant to his torturers until the servant settled the entire debt he owed the king.

Jesus used this parable to illustrate how foolish we look when we refuse to forgive our brother or sister for an offense when Jesus, our King, has forgiven us for so much more. Jesus commands us to open up, unlock our- selves, and forgive. He wants us to worship Him through our thanksgiving and forgive others as we find reasons to be thankful for and appreciative of them.

God cares about every facet of your life, including your bad and painful experiences. We must always remember that our present reactions that stem from past experiences affect our future solutions. Don't hold back your future solutions because of your refusal to unlock yourself, forgive, and then move forward. Unlock yourself and let God do what only He can do inside of you. Be free in Jesus' name.

Chapter 7

S = Suggest

"...let your requests be made known to God..."

It is amazing how clearly we perceive and understand when inner anxiety and outward conflict are no longer blocking our view of life. Some of our most innovative moments in life come when we are in a place of peace. That place of peace is called the play mode.

Once the unlock step is successfully executed, our conflict, offense, or pain should be resolved, forgiven, and healed. For many, this experience will be a joyous occasion to have peace restored back into your relationships. However, if we don't have a plan in place to ensure that the previous issues remain in the past, there is a good chance that we will repeat them.

Once we have successfully executed the steps of *Probe*, *Ask*, and *Unlock*, we should then complete the fourth step known as *Suggest*. Suggest means to make a proposal for a new habit to form. It means to recommend, give an idea, or to demonstrate. When we suggest, we elect to make a change to the current habit or method of operation that we currently have in place. If the current habit or method were effective, there would have been no need for us to activate the P.A.U.S.E. mode in the first place. The fact that P.A.U.S.E. was enabled serves as proof that the current practice was no longer effective.

Suggest is the root word of *suggestion*. Suggest is the initial thought in our minds to make a suggestion. Making a suggestion means to put our initial suggested thought into forward motion. A suggestion is an antidote that helps prevent a previous problem from reoccurring. When you make a suggestion after a conflict is resolved, you are setting a prayerful plan of action in place to correct and prevent the previous issue. You are letting your request be made known to whomever you were in conflict with, and you are letting your request be made known to God. You are giving that suggestion to God as well so that He can bear witness to the new suggestion and bless it. God loves to see conflicts resolved and honors and blesses us for doing so.

Suggestions that we make within the suggest step should be prayerful suggestions. They should be in sync with God's Word and His plans. Merely taking the ungodly suggestions of others can be a recipe for disaster.

Just because it may have worked for them, does not mean that it will work for you. If you haven't prayed over the suggestions you received from others, your suggestions are not blessed.

Again, making a suggestion is prayerfully making your own plan of action. It is great to seek the advice of others. However, once all of the suggestions are gathered, you should give those suggestions to God. You should let Him give you His thoughts on the matter as the final word. That is what it truly means to let your request be made known to Him.

Just as we don't have successful lives without proper planning, the same is true for relationships. We have to properly plan in order for them to work. They don't work themselves out on their own. Research has determined that only three percent of people in the United States take time to plan for their future. Yet, the three percent accomplish ten times more in their lifespan. Establishing goals and objectives in life are not suggestions; they are essential tools for success. It is mandatory that we establish goals in every area of our lives: our careers, personal lives, financial lives, family lives, and spiritual lives. The suggest step is about being intentional.

Proverbs 21:5 (NKJV) says, "The plans of the diligent lead surely to plenty, but those of everyone who is hasty, surely to poverty." Whether our relationships are plentiful or poor, are entirely up to our planning. If a particular plan is not working in our relationship, we need to change our plan. As the scripture suggests above, quick fixes seldom work. Take time to plan correctly. Your relationships deserve to be handled with care. There is a time to act fast and a time to act slow. The scripture above is not refuting that notion. It is simply stating that those who intentionally plan, produce far better results than those that don't.

When it comes to the suggest step, there are three things I believe we all should use to guide our suggestions to ensure that our plans are solid and productive. Those three things are: to count the cost first, to be proactive, and to remember that God has the final word.

Count the Cost First
Jesus said in Luke 14:28 (NKJV), "For which of you, intending to build a tower, does not sit down first and count the cost, whether he has enough to finish it?" When it comes to building effective relationships, much like building a tower, it is important for us to first consider how much we are willing to invest in that relationship. If the investment is little, one can expect a small return on

their investment. However, if the investment is a large sum, one can expect an exponentially large return.

Jesus was very clear in the scripture when He once said, "For with the measure you use, it will be measured to you." It is foolish for us to expect more out of a relationship than what we have put into it. It is important that we are honest up front in every relationship regarding our level of commitment. People are easily hurt when their level of commitment is far greater than what they expected in return. Clearly communicating and defining the level of commitment for both parties is vital to the success of any relationship.

A few other things to consider when counting the cost is to ask questions such as, "Can we accomplish this plan?" "Does this plan make sense for us?" "How will this decision impact our relationship and family?" and finally, the deciding factor, "Is this God's plan for us?"

Asking whether or not you can accomplish your plans is not always a lack of faith. Probing yourself to identify what resources you have available is a smart business decision. Remember Jesus said, "...which of you, intending to build a tower, does not sit down first and count the cost..." Asking yourself if whether or not you can accomplish your suggested plan is a sign of you being realistic, diligent, wise, and mature.

The suggestions or plans of action made in relationships should consider the opinions of all parties involved. Effective communication is not only about monologue; it is about dialogue. In fact, we can often add more value to others by allowing them to add more value to us. Counting the cost cannot properly be determined without first counting the value we find in others.

Be Proactive

We shouldn't just wait for conflict to happen; we should plan for it to happen. I didn't say we should always *expect* it to happen. I said we should *plan* for it, so in the event it does arise, we will know how to quickly resolve it before it escalates. Having insurance is a great example of having a suggestion or plan of action in place for unfortunate circumstances. We have insurance on numerous things we consider as our assets. We don't necessarily have the faith or desire to use our life insurance plans. No sane person wishes bad or harm upon themselves. Nevertheless, we have insurance in place to avoid our families and ourselves from experiencing a financial disaster in the event we experience a catastrophe. If your relationships are considered assets, you need to be proactive about having successful plans in place to ensure they are protected. You need an insurance plan.

Being more interactive is one of the best ways to come up with great suggestions or plans of action. Being a willing participant and not an idle observer goes a long way in life. Whenever we step out of our comfort zones and interact in areas that we do not normally function in, we learn, grow, and become better. Helping others with their assigned daily tasks is a great way to gain insight on their duties and develop more appreciation for their contribution. When doing so, we experience the same challenges they experience daily, which also allows us to then make suggestions to improve the process. It is often said, "Where there is no pain, there is no gain." True gain is about being proactive. It is about putting in the work.

Another way to develop great suggestions is to prepare ahead of time. There is a difference between planning ahead of time and preparing ahead of time. Planning means to design for the future, while preparing means to make ready for the future. A plan is just an idea if it doesn't eventually involve preparation. Proverbs 6:6-8 (NIV) says, "Go to the ant, you sluggard; consider its ways and be wise! It has no commander, no overseer or ruler, yet it stores its provision in summer and gathers its food at harvest." The ant doesn't just have a plan of action to store food; the ant is actually doing the preparation work as well. We have to plan for our relationships to work and then actually do the work.

Most people tend to be more reactive than proactive when it comes to dealing with conflict. When making suggestions, it is important that we are first proactive in doing our research on the topic concerning our conflict. We should be on the hunt for facts and truths that will support and help establish our suggestions. I cannot think of any greater truth or fact-checker than the Bible. The Bible is full of truths that are simple and practical to understand, yet powerful in revelation. When we make suggestions in a relationship, it is important that we make sure that our suggestions line-up with God's Word. Again, we get ourselves in a lot of trouble when we act on our own instincts or the advice of others without also prayerfully seeking God's direction. At the end of the day, if it doesn't line-up with God's Word, it doesn't line-up at all.

God Has the Final Word

I'm sure you've heard the saying before, "Right motive, wrong method." Most people in the world mean well when it comes to their relationships. Most people want to do right by people and treat them fairly. The challenge for most to maintain this truth is usually determined by how well they handle conflict.

Conflict has a way of influencing us to act irrational and out of character. It has a way of persuading us to make dumb decisions. Oftentimes, I see people look to fortune cookies, horoscopes, palm readers, TV, the internet, or even social media for advice on their relationships. Sure, there are times one might find sound advice on these forms of media. However, more often than not, the philosophies, opinions, or advice we receive through these avenues typically are wrong methods and are contrary to God's Word. A good idea can still be a bad idea if it isn't a God idea.

Proverbs 19:21 (NIV) says, "Many are the plans in a person's heart, but it is the Lord's purpose that prevails." This scripture doesn't mean God is over-controlling. This scripture actually shows how deep God's loves for us is and how interactive He wants to be in our lives. God doesn't want to just stand on the sidelines and watch us do life alone. He wants to influence our thoughts and desires, so we can make sound suggestions, proactive plans, and prepare our best lives. His plans for our lives prevail because He knows what is best for them. We often think we know what we want, but if that were true, we wouldn't change our minds so much.

When we let God have the final word in our lives, we communicate to God that we trust him. The suggest step is ineffective if we don't trust the person who is making the suggestions. Suggestions must come from a credible source; otherwise, they are merely opinions that we hear and will then ignore. Credibility is restored as we consistently prove that we can exercise sound judgment.

The suggest step ensures that we don't fall back into the same traps that tripped us up beforehand. The last place we want to end up is stuck in the rewind mode of life. When it comes to our suggestions, we have to be willing to count the cost first, be proactive, and then trust God's Word if we are going to be successful. I *suggest* you trust God to guide your plans. He has an undefeated record.

Chapter 8

E = Evaluate

"...and the peace of God, which surpasses all understanding, will guard your hearts and minds through Christ Jesus."

After a conflict is resolved by walking through the steps of: *Probe, Ask, Unlock,* and *Suggest,* you should finally *Evaluate* your suggestions. The word *"evaluate"* means to follow-up, assess, examine, analyze, judge, rate, appraise, or also check the temperature. The evaluate step is a defensively-minded step. It is slightly different from the probe step which is again, more offensively minded. The evaluate step seeks to prevent and avoid conflict at all possible costs. The probe step proactively steps in to identify and examine a conflict once it has already risen. Again, the probe step is the first step when initiating the P.A.U.S.E. mode.

For example, a train's caboose is designed to keep a lookout for potential threatening issues. It also serves as a place for train crew members to relax in peace while the rest of the train is powered forward by the train's front engine. *Probe* is the front engine of the P.A.U.S.E. mode, while *Evaluate* is its caboose. Much like a caboose, God's place of peace and understanding comes from His Word. God promises us that He will guide our hearts and minds through His Word, and His Word is Jesus Christ. When our suggestions are evaluated through the eyes of Christ, pure motives and plans are perceived. Our suggestions, plans, and habits must be evaluated through God's Word.

Evaluate Your Habits

Evaluating is about following up with your newly proposed suggestions or habits to ensure that you remain consistent with them until they become permanent habits. Studies have shown that it takes 21 days to create a new habit. It then takes another 21 days to strengthen your resolve to embed that habit so that your poor habits cannot overpower it. Finally, it takes another 21 days to make sure your new habit remains a permanent part of your DNA forever. In other words, breaking an old habit, creating a new habit, and making it a permanent habit in your life is a 63-day process on average.

The above research explains why we so often find ourselves back in situations that we really do not desire to be. Just think of how many times you said you were not going to do something again, only to find yourself right back in the thick of it. How many New Year's reso- lutions have you broken? How about the treadmill at home that is collecting dust even though you swore to yourself you were going to use it this year? Why is main- taining that diet or workout plan so difficult? The chances are, if it involves your flesh (your body), you are going to experience some level of resistance.

The Apostle Paul experienced this firsthand when he wrote in Romans 7:14-20 (NKJV), "For we know that the law is spiritual, but I am carnal, sold under sin. For what I am doing, I do not understand. For what I will to do, that I do not practice; but what I hate, that I do. If, then, I do what I will not to do, I agree with the law that it is good. But now, it is no longer I who do it, but sin that dwells in me. For I know that in me (that is, in my flesh) nothing good dwells; for to will is present with me, but how to perform what is good, I do not find. For the good that I will to do, I do not do; but the evil I will not to do, that I practice. Now if I do what I will not to do, it is no longer I who do it, but sin that dwells in me."

How is that for transparency? Paul who was a well-known preacher of the gospel, active follower of Christ, and a church leader was admitting that he had bad habits that he struggled to break and overcome. Deliverance cannot occur until we are honest enough to admit what our struggles are. There is power in evaluating our bad habits and calling them what they are. When we rationalize or justify them, we stunt our own spiritual and emotional growth.

Paul said that whatever we do without faith is sin (Romans 14:23). Faith means to have complete trust or confidence in someone or something. Do you have complete trust or confidence in your bad habits? If not, chances are you are sinning against your body when you continue to practice a habit you lack faith in. The Bible is clear in stating that our bodies are the temple for the Holy Spirit to dwell within us (1 Cor. 6:19). If we knew Christ was coming to our house to live with us, would we keep it dirty or would we keep it clean for His arrival? We only fool ourselves and short-circuit our destinies when we live beneath our privileges. God is not mocked; we reap what we sow.

Notice that Paul said in the Romans text above, "I do what I will not to do." However, he didn't just stop there and accept his bad habits. He then evaluated himself to identify where his thoughts and actions stem from. He later stated that he found that God's law is good; therefore, he concluded that it is the sin inside of him that is influencing his bad habits. Are your relationships struggling because of the sin that still dwells within you? Do you keep trying to justify that bad habit? Do you think just because your sin is a secret it doesn't outwardly affect your relationships? It wasn't until the next chapter that Paul wrote that he realizes that he is free and under no more condemnation when he is in Christ. Why wait until the next chapter of your life to be set free? You can be set free today if you are willing to surrender your bad habits to Christ.

Evaluate your Faith

We should constantly evaluate our faith to ensure we are living our life predominately in the play mode. Remember, whatever we do without faith is sin. Sin moves us out of the play mode of life. It is so easy to get stuck in the rewind, fast-forward, and stop modes of life. Living in the past, getting too far ahead of ourselves, or quitting on life is far too easy to practice. When we make a suggestion in a relationship, we should have faith that our new habit is going to work. Again, having faith is about having complete confidence or trust. God does not want us to live a life of doubt. He wants us to walk by our faith and not by what we see. He wants us to be sure of ourselves.

The information that we receive through the various outlets of media can create anxiety, stress, or anger if we're not careful. However, God does not want us to solely rely on our view of the world. He wants us to see the world through His view and love each other through His love. We often defeat ourselves before we ever get started because of our lack of faith. If we make a suggestion but do not evaluate our faith in that decision, we are just wasting our time. Our suggestion is propelled forward by our faith. Our suggestion is the car; however, our faith is the engine underneath the hood. If you turn on your faith, your suggestion will successfully move forward. Make it a point to regularly evaluate your faith.

Evaluate Your Vision

Accurately evaluating your suggestions also requires you to evaluate your vision. Any suggestion that does not have a vision attached to it will eventually lose the air under its wings. Proverbs 29:18 (NKJV) says, "Where there is no revelation, the people cast off restraint." Revelation is the act of disclosing something previously secret or obscure. It means bringing to light what was wholly hidden. Revelation is a divine or supernatural disclosure to humans. It is a surprising or previously unknown fact. Restraint is the control over the expression of one's emotions or thoughts. It means self-control, self-discipline, or moderation. When we restrain ourselves, we keep ourselves under control or within our set limits.

When our relationships lack a healthy element of surprise, openness, honesty, and revelation, we are compelled to cast off restraint. Being self-controlled or self-discipline becomes a challenge when we lose hope. We hope for surprises, not plain, predictable things. If your relationships are boring, dull, or unfulfilling, you need to evaluate the vision you have in place. If you don't have a healthy vision, you won't have a healthy relationship.

God loves us so much that He wants to give us a vision of ourselves in every relationship that we are involved in. He wants us to experience the true peace that is not influenced by life circumstances. He desires us to have the peace that surpasses this world's understanding. Many relationships struggle to have peace because they do not have God's divine revelation for their relationship. We all have our own ideas and our own ways that we constantly try to force on others. We have our own vision of each other, rather than the vision that God has for us. When you evaluate yourself and ask God to show you who He desires you to be, He will take you on quite a journey. He will reveal to you some areas of improvement. He will show you where you can improve with helping out or contribute more in your relationships. He will even show you where you have been wrong. However, He will also show you things you do well and should keep doing. He will give you His revelation for your life.

Whether you are a son, daughter, father, mother, husband, wife, or friend, God wants to give you His vision and revelation for your relationships. He wants to give you His suggestions and show you the plans He has just for you. All you have to do is evaluate your vision and then walk in it. He has already written the story; you just have to live it out. However, in order to live it out, you have to continue to follow-up on the plans you allowed Him to make for you.

Evaluate Your Follow-Up

As mentioned earlier, studies have shown that it takes 21 days to create a new habit. It takes another 21 days to strengthen your resolve to embed that habit so your poor habits cannot overpower it. Lastly, it takes another 21 days to make it a permanent habit. Based on this information, it is clear that if we want to form new habits in our lives, following up is key to our success. You must *evaluate your follow-up.*

Follow-up is a continuation or repetition of something that has already been started or done. It means to conduct a further observation of an active suggestion or plan of action. Following up on our suggestions after a conflict is not only a great practice; it is mandatory if we are going to break our bad habits or vicious cycle we often find ourselves in.

Sadly, there are many reasons why we choose not to follow-up with our suggestions, new habits, or goals in life. One of the main reasons is pretty simple, we forget. It's easy to forget things in life considering how busy we are. Work, school, children, church, dance recitals and sporting events are enough things to keep our hands tied and heads spinning by the end of the day. We might have every intention to follow-up on a suggestion we made; however, our busy lives somehow often seem to overpower that ambition.

On other occasions, we'll remember our suggestion. However, the other party may continuously forget the suggestion. When this happens, we often eventually let the suggestion fade away so that we won't appear too pushy. Usually, false assumptions accompany our refusal to appear pushy. We usually will start to assume the worst and convince ourselves that the other party doesn't care or respect us. What else could be the reason for them forgetting, right? The fact is, just because someone forgets doesn't always mean that they don't care or respect you. Sometimes, they are simply busy themselves, or they are even perhaps stumped on how to continue moving the suggestion forward.

One of the most common myths that following-up falls prey to is the thought from people that after a conflict is resolved, everything will just work itself out. This is a lie the devil tries to convince us to believe so that we can become complacent and fall back into our lives of mediocrity. Whatever has value requires work to maintain its value.

Follow-up is about being intentional. It does not mean we are being pushy or overly concerned. It means that you care enough to consistently check-in on your relationships and ensure that a healthy balance still remains. When it comes to checking the remaining balance in your bank account, do you just say to yourself, "I won't check it, it will just work itself out?" If you're financially responsible, you wouldn't dare think of such a thing. If you're relationally responsible, you wouldn't dare think that way either. Just as finances do not maintain or grow themselves, relationships do not either. Following up is not just a good practice; it is essential.

When it comes to follow-up, a few questions to ask yourself might be:

- Is this suggestion or new habit still beneficial?
- Are we still holding ourselves accountable?
- Are we still actively practicing the suggestion?
- Is the suggestion in place Biblical and practical?

Holding ourselves accountable and allowing others we trust to hold us accountable is all part of the evaluate step. No one can nor should they do life alone. We are all created to interact with each other. We were born to make a difference and our imprint together in this world. God's design is that we do it together in harmony and through His love. Self-made notions are from the devil. There is no such thing as a self-made person. All of us needed someone else to help create us, including Adam and Eve.

Evaluate your relationships through your follow-up. Don't allow complacency to set in your relationships. Instead, cherish, nurture, and grow your relationships by consistently evaluating the health of them. The world will know that we value our relationships when they evaluate the way that we love each other. When we effectively do this, we show the world the love of Christ.

Chapter 9

Mastering the Art of the P.A.U.S.E.

"If I speak in the tongues of men or of angels, but do not have love, I am only a resounding gong or a clanging cymbal"- 1 Corinthians 13:1 (NIV)

Congratulations, if you have made it this far, that means you have learned about all five steps of the P.A.U.S.E. mode. Now that you know what each step means, I want to discuss some practical, Biblical wisdom you can use to apply the P.A.U.S.E. mode in your everyday communicative situations. I called this process: *"Mastering the Art of the P.A.U.S.E."*

The beauty of the P.A.U.S.E. mode is how it can be applied at any time, during any situation, and with anyone. For example, you can use it yourself when you have an internal conflict due to inner anxiety. You can apply it in order to prevent potential arguments in any relationship, whether they are intimate or platonic in nature. Finally, the P.A.U.S.E. mode can be applied in the middle of a conflict, long after you may have forgotten to initially apply it.

Whenever you find yourself in a conflict, whether it is within yourself or with someone else, take time to go into the P.A.U.SE. mode. Remember, the word *"pause"* represents a brief interruption, breathing space, hesitation, thinking carefully, and reflection. Take time to think carefully, reflect, and examine the situation before merely reacting. Ask yourself, how would Christ handle this situation? What does the Bible say about this situation? Is there anyone that I know who could provide sound, Biblical advice or counsel? Wasn't that the whole point of the W.W.J.D. bracelets when they first came out? Wasn't it meant to remind you to ask yourself, "What would Jesus do?" The P.A.U.S.E. mode not only reminds you to ask what Jesus would have done; it also walks you through the five steps to help you resolve any situation that hinders you from walking in love.

Again, the P.A.U.S.E. mode is founded on Philippians 4:6-7 (NKJV) which says, "Be anxious for nothing, but in everything by prayer and supplication, with thanksgiving, let your requests be made known to God; and the peace of God, which surpasses all understanding, will guard your hearts and minds through Christ Jesus." Instead of letting anxiety overcome you, the Bible says to pray (Probe). It says use supplication (Ask) and do it with thanksgiving so that you can open up and heal any wound (Unlock). It says to let your request be made known to God (Suggest), and the peace of God through Christ Jesus will show you how to guard your hearts and minds through your follow-up (Evaluate).

One of the things that I love most about the evaluate step is that it is always on the defense against conflict. It doesn't look for conflict or fault in others. It is not judgmental or parades itself around in a self-righteous way looking to condemn people who are struggling with sin. It simply alerts our minds when conflict is potentially threatening us so we can enable the P.A.U.S.E. mode again. Even though the probe step looks for conflicts, it is not done to cause strife or to pick a fight. It is done out of love to guard and protect us and those who we are in relationship with. God is so good He has us covered on both ends!

Live your life in the play mode until God presses the stop button on your life and calls you home. Never press your own stop button on your life. That button is reserved for God and God only. When life becomes overwhelming, activate the P.A.U.S.E. mode and walk through the steps so you can get back to living life in the play mode. If you want to press stop on something in life, press stop on anxiety, fear, doubt, depression, frustration, stress, worry, jealousy, bitterness, and resentment. Resolve in your mind that you will not live another day with any more regrets holding you back again. *Master the Art of the P.A.U.S.E.*, and you will master your mind.

P.A.U.S.E. Renews the Mind

The P.A.U.S.E. mode is a manner of renewing the mind to think about how to appropriately respond rather than to negatively react. Romans 12:2 (NKJV) says, "And do not be conformed to this world, but be transformed by the renewing of your mind, that you may prove what is that good and acceptable and perfect will of God." When Paul wrote this scripture, he was informing the church to not be conformed to this world. He was saying that we should not think with the same mindset as the world. We have God's Word to guide and protect us.

When we conform to the world, we comply with its rules, standards, or laws. God is not telling us to disobey the laws of this world; He is telling us to obey both His Word and the laws of the world. However, any law, person, or thing in this world that is contrary to what His

Word says must not be followed. When we adopt the ways of this world, we make ourselves enemies of God.

God's Word and law precedes any laws on earth. That is what Paul means by not being conformed to this world. Any form of media controlled by the laws and standards of this world, and not by God's Word, must be rejected. Any media-controlled influence that creates inner anxiety within our minds should be filtered out.

2 Corinthians 10:4-6 (NKJV) says, "For the weapons of our warfare are not carnal but mighty in God for pulling down strongholds, casting down arguments and every high thing that exalts itself against the knowledge of God, bringing every thought into captivity to the obedience of Christ, and being ready to punish all disobedience when your obedience is fulfilled." The best way to punish disobedience is through our obedience to Christ. If you want to show the world that your way of living is right, live a life that pleases God.

A renewed mind is a dangerous mind. It is a threat to the ways of this world and a threat to the enemy. A renewed mind disapproves the ways of this world and exposes it's wrong and sinful nature simply through our example of living a Christ-filled life. Sinners are not persuaded to repent through someone standing on the street corner with a bullhorn telling them that they are going to

131

hell. They are persuaded by the grace that we show them and the grace we show towards other believers. Our best testimony is to show the world how to properly respond to each other during conflict. The P.A.U.S.E. mode does just that through the steps of responding through love. Jesus said in John, Chapter 13 that the world will know that we are His disciples by the way we love each other. True love comes through a renewed mind.

There are a lot of agendas today being pushed throughout various forms of media in an attempt to influence our thoughts, feelings, and actions. We must be vigilant in identifying such agendas, filtering them through God's Word, keeping the good, and rejecting the bad. God expects nothing less from us. We're either hot or cold for Him. We are for Him or against Him. A lukewarm Christian is the worst of all because they do not exemplify faith. It is time for us to make a choice, whether we are for Christ or not. It's time to make a choice, whether we want to live a life of love or fear. The time to decide is now.

Biggest Stumbling Blocks
Maybe you're thinking, this all sounds great, however, who in the relationship should initiate the P.A.U.S.E. mode when conflict arises? Great question. Let's look to the scripture for that answer. Jesus said in Matthew 23:11

(NIV), "The greatest among you will be your servant." In other words, whoever considers themselves the most mature should be the one to initiate the P.A.U.S.E. mode. The person who considers themselves as the smartest, strongest, and emotionally stable, congratulations, you get to apologize first!

One of the biggest stumbling blocks to the P.A.U.S.E. mode is forgetting to actually P.A.U.S.E. when conflicts threaten. Oh, the joy we'd have if we can only learn to maintain our cool during heated situations. Think of all of the trouble we would avoid and peace we would re- tain. It is so easy to forget to P.A.U.S.E. in order to prevent and resolve conflict when we are not walking prayerfully (or consistently probing). Fortunately, if we forget to activate the P.A.U.S.E. mode and find ourselves in the middle of a conflict, all we have to do is activate it wherever we are and work through the steps. It works, whether we initially remember it or not. However, walking prayerfully will enable us to activate the P.A.U.S.E. mode sooner rather than later.

Paul said we should always "pray without ceasing." Prayer can be done with our eyes open, while we're sitting in a chair, driving a car, running, or even walking. Prayer is a spiritual cellphone programmed inside of us. Prayer is simply talking with God.

Cellphones are a great blessing and a wonderful invention. However, if not managed correctly, they can be a huge stumbling block to our communication with God. If you wake up in the morning and you view what's happening on social media before you speak with God, your cellphone is a stumbling block. If you spend more time reading social media posts or blogs, watching TV, or listening to music (even Christian music) instead of praying or studying God's word, those things are stumbling blocks. Even though Christian music is incredibly uplifting and encouraging, it should never be substituted for communication with God.

Excessive pride is another big stumbling block to the P.A.U.S.E. mode. Proverbs 16:18 (NIV) says, "Pride goes before destruction, a haughty spirit before a fall." When we think we know everything and nobody can tell us anything, our fall is on its way. When we refuse to heed wise counsel and do things another way, even though we know our way is wrong, our fall is on its way. When we refuse to give grace and forgive our offenders, our fall is on its way.

It is good to have a sense of pride that represents our dignity and self-respect. Having pride is not a bad thing; excessive pride is the problem. Being excessively prideful is a great problem many people struggle to overcome.

Pride separates us, renders us unteachable, closes our minds, prevents us from admitting mistakes, encourages poor character decisions, holds us back from reaching our goals, and destroys our relationships. It makes us conceited, arrogant, and gives us a false sense of entitlement.

Pride is self-centered and incredibly destructive. The last thing someone who is prideful wants to do in the event of a conflict is pause. Prideful people wait for no one. They speak their own minds whenever they want and state that they're just keeping it real. Yeah, they're keeping it real alright…real dumb. Proverbs 29:11 (NKJV) says, "A fool vents all of his feelings, but a wise man holds them back." The P.A.U.S.E. mode keeps us from keeping it real dumb.

Oftentimes, taking a second to just pause alone keeps us out of trouble or from saying something we'll later regret. Making the effort to bite our lip and not fire back an unloving comment goes a long way. Imagine if Jesus fired back at us whenever He felt like we said something foolish or were out of line. How would you feel about Him then? You'd probably still love Him, but if He kept being overly critical of you, that love would start to dissipate. That is how we are when we choose to complain and criticize others for their faults all of the time.

There is nothing wrong with bringing up issues, as long as they are communicated through love. In fact, the P.A.U.S.E. mode encourages issues to be brought into the forefront. The P.A.U.S.E. mode is not some weak or wimpy formula to degrade women or emasculate men. The P.A.U.S.E. mode is powerful, and it works every time when executed properly. The P.A.U.S.E. mode was created from God's Word, and His Word does not return back void but always prospers in whatever it was spoken to do.

Sometimes you may experience a prideful person who refuses to embrace the steps of P.A.U.S.E. as you walk through them. Perhaps they are too upset to talk to you, or they are screaming and cursing at you. Getting them to unlock themselves in this situation is a bit of a long-shot. So what do you do? If we activate the probe step or are walking prayerfully, we will remember what Paul said in Ephesians 4:26 (NIV), "In your anger do not sin: Do not let the sun go down while you are still angry, and do not give the devil a foothold."

It is hard to walk and move forward when the devil has a hold of our feet. Have you ever noticed how hard it is to pray, read your Bible, or get anything done when you are angry with someone? That is because the devil has a firm grip on your spiritual feet. He is keeping you from moving forward. He wants you out of the play mode and stuck in the stop or rewind mode. When we find ourselves in this situation, the key is to remember the P.A.U.S.E. mode. Instead of being anxious and saying or doing something silly that we will later regret, we need to pray (probe). We need to ask God to give us His wisdom (ask). We need to thank God for that person, even though it may be hard at that time (unlock ourselves). We should let our request be made known to God (suggest). When this is done from a sincere heart, ungrudgingly, God will follow through and bestow His love and peace upon us, give us His guidance, and work on the other person's heart (evaluate). Nobody can straighten someone else out better than God.

Sometimes the evaluate step is about you identifying that you have done all that you can, and you have to trust God to resolve the rest. Again, when we refuse to carry out these steps, we are letting our pride get in the way. When we ask for forgiveness or choose to forgive from a sincere heart, the power shifts in our favor. It doesn't make us weaker; it actually makes us more powerful — the pressure shifts away from us and onto the other party involved. If the ask step is properly executed from a sincere, humble heart and earnestly done, the Holy Spirit will convict the other party through love. Love never fails.

Conflict Mastered by Love

When we walk in love, we walk in God's footsteps because God is love. I wrote this entire book, that is full of Biblical principles, in order to help you resolve any conflicts in your life. However, the truth is, if you do not have love for God, His Word, and His people, you will fail miserably over and over again. Your work and effort will be in vain, and it will not matter. You will frustrate yourself and revert back to old unproductive habits.

1 Corinthians 13:1 (NIV) says, "If I speak in the tongues of men or angels, but do not have love, I am only a resounding gong or a clanging cymbal." Love is familiar. We often become very familiar with those whom we love. Unfortunately, our complacency and familiarity with each other often influences us to become impatient, boastful, proud, or judgmental toward one another. The fact that we know each other so well can be a plus or minus, depending on our perspectives.

No one in the world can upset us like our spouse, family member, or close friend can. It is that very closeness that allows us to become so familiar that respect and formality are often forgotten. Because we know them so well, we typically tend to stop being so formal or treating them with respect. It becomes quite easy to overlook their needs and disregard their feelings. Shifting from formal to informal in a close relationship is perfectly fine and natural. However, respect should always remain at the forefront of any relationship. When we don't feel respected, we don't feel loved.

Also notice that Paul said in 1 Corinthians 13:11 (NIV), "When I was a child, I talked like a child, I thought like a child, I reasoned like a child. When I became a man, I put the ways of childhood behind me." Real love is fully grown and mature. It is not arrogant, prideful, sarcastic, boastful, rude, or overly sensitive. Those are all childish and immature ways. When we were children, we screamed from the top of our lungs, lost self-control, or physically fought when we didn't get our way. We pouted, threw tantrums, and took verbal jabs at each other. However, now that we have grown into adulthood, we look silly acting this way in relationships. Getting mad and storming out of the door should be a thing of the past. Being mad at each other for days and weeks is childish. Standing and facing our conflicts the same day in the heat of the battle is what true warriors do.

Mastering the Art of the P.A.U.S.E. teaches us to act in a mature and responsible way. It is time-out for all of the bickering and fighting within your relationships. Instead, take a time-out to P.A.U.S.E. so you can press time-in on your figurative play button of life and get back to living in perfect harmony. Conflict is mastered by love. If we are not filled with love when we choose to activate the P.A.U.S.E. mode, we will crash and burn. Our arguments will sound like a resounding gong or clanging cymbals. We won't be able to understand each other.

Galatians 6:7 (NIV) says, "Do not be deceived: God cannot be mocked. A man reaps what he sows." What are you sowing? Are you sowing love or hate? Are you sowing arrogance and judgment or grace and mercy? Whatever it is that you sow, that is exactly what is coming back to you. I'm always amazed at people who complain, gossip, curse at people, yell, or sow hateful things; however, they are offended when someone is unloving towards them. If you produce and sow negativity in your life, you will receive it back from others. God is not mocked.

The Bible expresses in James, Chapter 3 that our mouths contain an untamed tongue. We can tame animals, birds, reptiles, and sea creatures, but we can't tame the tongue. We all need grace when it comes to our mouths. Stop holding your spouse, family member, co-worker or friend to unreasonable standards. James said in this very chapter that if any of us are never at fault in what we say, we would be perfect. Are any of us perfect? With that said, cut your relationships some slack. Understand that every now and again, people are going to slip up and say something offensive, and so are you! Extend grace and mercy in these situations knowing that one day, you will need that same grace and mercy. Sow it now so you can receive it later. Don't hide from conflict anymore. Don't react in a childish, immature, or unloving way. The next time conflict threatens, react with grace and mercy. Extend grace to the untamed tongue. Take time to pause and then activate the P.A.U.S.E. mode.

Mastering the Art of the P.A.U.S.E. cannot be mastered any other way except through love. It is possible to master your relationships with others. It is possible to live your life predominately in the play mode of life, enjoying the great things that life offers. Once we master the art of loving each other as ourselves, we will Master the Art of the P.A.U.S.E.

www.ingramcontent.com/pod-product-compliance
Lightning Source LLC
Chambersburg PA
CBHW060937040426
42445CB00011B/903